The Gospel of Mark

An Expository Outline

Hamilton Smith

Scripture Truth Publications

THE GOSPEL OF MARK

Paperback edition first published 1981 by Central Bible Hammond Trust Limited, Wooler.

Transferred to Digital Printing 2007

ISBN: 978-0-901860-69-9 (paperback)

ISBN: 978-0-901860-70-5 (hardback)

© Copyright 2007 Scripture Truth

Published by Scripture Truth Publications
Coopies Way, Coopies Lane,
Morpeth, Northumberland, NE61 6JN

Scripture Truth is an imprint of Central Bible Hammond Trust, a charitable trust

Typesetting by John Rice
Printed and bound by Lightning Source

Contents

THE GOSPEL OF MARK

Introduction

God, in His goodness, having given us the history of our Lord Jesus Christ, in His journey through this world, we have a reliable, because inspired, account of events in which the eternal destiny of each one is involved. Moreover, through this account, God would have our hearts attracted to the living Christ as the all varied glories of His life, and death, and resurrection, pass before us.

To appreciate these glories God would have us discern the different relationships in which Christ may be viewed, as well as the varied characters in which He is presented. To this end we have four Gospels, each giving a distinct presentation of the glory of Christ. The study of the gospel of Matthew clearly shows that the special details that are given in connection with the incidents, as well as the teaching, have in view the presentation of the Lord Jesus as the long promised Messiah — the Son of David, in connection with Israel.

In the gospel of Luke it is equally plain that the Lord Jesus is presented as the Son of Man, making known the grace of God to a world of needy sinners.

In the gospel of John we have the presentation of His divine glory as the Son of God.

In the gospel of Mark, the whole record is consistent with the presentation of the Lord Jesus as the Servant of Jehovah, serving others in love. Centuries before the coming of Christ, Isaiah had foretold that the Lord Jesus would come into the world as the Servant of Jehovah, for the word of the LORD came to the prophet saying, "Behold *my Servant*, whom I uphold; mine elect, in whom my soul delighteth; I will put my spirit upon Him He shall bring forth judgment to the Gentiles" (Isaiah 42:1). All the details of this gospel have in view the presentation of His perfect service for needy man, as the Servant of Jehovah carrying out His will.

1.
The Preparation of the Way of the Lord

CHAPTER 1:1-20

In the gospel of Mark the Holy Spirit presents the Lord Jesus in all His lowly grace as the Servant of Jehovah. Nevertheless, we are ever to remember that the One who stoops to become the obedient Servant never ceases to be Who He is, as a Divine Person, because of what He became as a lowly Servant in the likeness of men. Thus, to guard His glory, the gospel opens with a sevenfold witness to the greatness of His Person.

VERSE 1

The first witness is the writer of the Gospel. Mark, who is used by the Holy Spirit to bring before us the One who made Himself of no reputation, and took upon Him the form of a servant, opens his gospel by reminding us that He is "Jesus Christ, the Son of God".

VERSES 2-3

Secondly, the prophets are quoted, as bearing witness to the glory of His Person. They not only foretell His coming, but they announce His glory. Jehovah's word to

Malachi is, "Behold, I will send my messenger, and he shall prepare the way before *Me*." The Spirit applies these words to Christ, for He says, "Behold, I send my messenger before *thy face*, which shall prepare *thy way*." Jesus of the New Testament is the Jehovah of the Old Testament (Malachi 3:1). The second quotation from Isaiah speaks of preparing the way of the LORD. Thus again it is Jehovah whose way is prepared — for Jesus is Jehovah (Isaiah 40:3).

VERSES 4-8

Thirdly, we have the witness of John, the Forerunner, to the glory of the perfect Servant. On the one hand, he bears witness to the sinful condition of man, and the need of "repentance for the remission of sins"; on the other hand, he witnesses to the glory of the One who had come in lowly grace as the Servant to meet man's need. He takes his stand in the wilderness, "and there went out to him all the land of Judaea, and they of Jerusalem". Long centuries before, the Lord had said to the prophet, "Behold, I will allure her, and bring her into the wilderness, and speak to her heart" (Hosea 2:14). As one has said, "There was no talking to her heart … in the fair and flourishing city …; but out in the cold, hungry, waste wilderness, He allured her", there to speak to the conscience and win the heart. And to-day how often this way is taken with sinners, and, indeed with saints. We seek comfort and ease, too often to find our hearts growing cold and careless; then the Lord breaks in on our ease with sorrow and trial, in order to speak to our hearts and attract us to Himself.

Appealing to the conscience, John shows that our sins have turned the fair creation into a moral wilderness, and separated man from God. His manner of life, lived apart from the world, was in consistency with his testimony. Above all, he bore witness to the glory of the One that was coming. If the One who "thought it not robbery to be equal with God", stoops to become a Man, and takes the form of a servant, John, the greatest among prophets, delights to own that a yet greater Servant has come, the latchet of whose shoes he is not worthy to unloose. John may, indeed, baptize with water, and by this sign of death separate people from their former associations with a corrupt world, but Jesus will baptize with the Holy Ghost — a Divine Person — the seal that henceforth believers belong to Christ in a new world.

VERSES 9-11

Fourthly, we have the witness of the voice from Heaven to the glory of Christ. In infinite grace the Lord submits to baptism, thus identifying Himself with the godly remnant in separation from the guilty nation. Straightway the Father's voice is heard declaring His glory as the "beloved Son", the One in whom the Father finds His delight. Already, in days of old, Jehovah had said by the prophet, "Behold my Servant ... in whom my soul delighteth: I will put my Spirit upon Him" (Isaiah 42:1). Thus the voice from heaven can say, "My Servant" is "My beloved Son". It has been truly said, He was "sealed by the Holy Spirit even as we are; *He*, because He was personally worthy of it; *we*, because He has made us worthy by His work and by His blood" (J. N. Darby).

VERSES 12-13

Fifthly, we have a brief allusion to the temptation in the wilderness. The temptation of our first parents in a garden of delights brought out their weakness whereby they were overcome by Satan. The temptation of our Lord, in a wilderness, became a witness to His infinite perfection, whereby He overcame Satan.

Sixthly, creation, itself, bears witness to the glory of His Person, for we read, He was *"with the wild beasts"*. However much the beasts may fear men, they have no fear of this blessed Man, for He, indeed, is their Creator.

Lastly, we read, "the Angels ministered unto Him." The One who came to be the Servant is, Himself, served by angelic hosts. He is none less than "the Son", "the First Begotten", of Whom, when He comes into the world, it is said, "Let all the angels of God worship Him" (Hebrews 1:5, 6).

Thus, in their various seasons, heaven and earth, prophets and angels, declare the glory of Jesus as a Divine Person and so prepare the way of the Lord for the lowly place He was about to take as the Servant among men.

It will be noticed that, in this gospel, no genealogy is given, and no details of His birth, or circumstances of His early life are recorded. These details, so precious and needed, duly recorded by others, would hardly be in keeping with either the Gospel of Mark or John. Here, as the Servant, He takes a place beneath all genealogies, whereas, in the gospel of John, as the Son, He takes a place above all human genealogies.

Following upon this sevenfold witness to the glory of His Person, we have, in these introductory verses, the record of the event that prepared the way of the Lord to enter upon His public service, the character of His service, and the sovereign grace that chose others to be His companions in service.

VERSE 14

It is significant that it was after John had been "put in prison" that Jesus came forth to serve. Nature might argue that if the Forerunner is rejected it will be useless for Jesus to proceed with His mission. But God's times, and ways, of action, are very different to those of men. The ministry of John, as indeed the rejection of John, was a demonstration of man's sin and need; but this only prepared the way for, and proved the need of, a ministry of grace that alone can meet the need. When the world proved its sin by rejecting John, God declared His grace by sending Jesus.

VERSE 15

The great end of the Lord's service, as recorded in the Gospel of Mark, is summed up in this verse. He was present in the midst of Israel to proclaim that the Kingdom of God had drawn nigh — a Kingdom marked by righteousness, peace, and joy (Romans 14:17). Already, John had come in the way of righteousness, convicting men of their sins; now the Lord was present — not to judge men for their sins, — but in grace, calling men to repent in view of the glad tidings that proclaims the forgiveness of sins.

VERSES 16-20

We then learn the grace of the Lord that identifies others with Himself in service. He passes by the official priests, the learned scribes, and the religious Pharisees, and takes up humble fishermen. Simon is one who can say, "Silver and gold have I none", and of whom the world said he was an "unlearned and ignorant man" (Acts 3:6; 4:13). The lack of riches and human learning is no hindrance to being a companion of the Lord, or to being used in His service. Nevertheless, however humble the calling of those the Lord may engage in His service, they are not unemployed. These simple men were pursuing their occupation of fishermen, when the Lord called them to become *fish-*

ers of men. The Lord's service is not to be taken up by those who have nothing else to do.

Moreover, His servants need to be fitted for service, and this training can only be effected by being in His company; therefore, the Lord's word is "Come ye after Me, and I will make you to become fishers of men." This is still true, for the Lord's word remains, "If any man serve Me, let him *follow Me*" (John 12:26). Alas! we may be content with believing the gospel for the benefit of our souls, and know little of going on to follow the Lord in the path of faith and lowly obedience that prepares the way for service. We may not be called to literally forsake all, as with the disciples when the Lord was present on earth, but if we are to serve Him it can only be as, in spirit, He becomes the blessed Object before the soul. All may not be called to surrender their daily calling. This, indeed, is only the path of a few. The majority of God's people are definitely told to remain in their earthly calling (1 Corinthians 7:20). Nevertheless the Lord has some service for all, for "Unto *every one* is given grace according to the measure of the gift of Christ" (Ephesians 4:7). This service will involve the surrender of all those things that would entangle us in the affairs of this life, and can only be carried out as we keep near to Him. On the part of these disciples there was an immediate response to the Lord's call, for we read, they "followed Him", and again they "went after Him".

2.
The Perfect Servant

The Lord's way has been prepared and the companions in His path of service have been chosen. In the portion that follows we have the record of certain incidents that very blessedly set forth the perfect Servant. In the glory of His Person He must ever be alone; but in His service we have the perfect pattern for any servant of the Lord. Peter gives us a very beautiful epitome of the Gospel of Mark when he says, "God anointed Jesus of Nazareth with the Holy Ghost and with power; who went about doing good, and healing all that were oppressed of the devil, for God was with Him" (Acts 10:38). We, indeed, are not called to perform miracles of healing, for in a day of failure the Church has been shorn of her ornaments; but in the *manner* of His service we are called to follow Him.

VERSES 21-22

Accompanied by His disciples the Lord entered the synagogue at Capernaum and taught on the sabbath day. At once we see an outstanding mark of the perfect Servant, for we read, in contrast to the scribes "He taught as one that had *authority*". His word did not consist of mere arguments that appeal to reason, but He spake with the authority of One who proclaims the truth in convicting power. In our day, and measure, we are to use any God-given gift with authority, for, says Peter in his Epistle, "If any man speak, let him speak as the oracles of God" (1 Peter 4:10, 11). If we present doctrines with all the arguments for and against, leaving our hearers to judge whether it be truth or not, we shall hardly be speaking with authority, but rather as those who are groping for the truth. We are to speak as those who by grace, know the certainty of the truth they proclaim. This is not inconsistent with the lowly mind, for indeed it is the lowly that will know the mind of God, as we read, "The meek will He teach His way" (Psalm 25:9).

VERSES 23-28

The casting out of the unclean spirit makes manifest another mark of the perfect Servant. If He speaks with authority, His word carries *power*. In the place of religious profession there was a man with an unclean spirit. The presence of Jesus is intolerable to such; thus, "he cried out, saying, Let us alone." Whatever the ignorance of man, the demons know that this lowly Servant — Jesus of Nazareth — is none less than the Son of God. The Lord, however, will have no witness borne to Himself by the Devil. Thus He rebukes the demon, silences him, and commands him to come out of the man. The demon having shewn his power over the man by tearing him, and crying with a loud voice, has to submit to the yet greater power of the Lord by coming out of the man.

The audience, already astonished that He taught with authority, are now amazed at *the power* that accompanied His word of authority, to which even unclean spirits have to submit.

VERSES 29-34

Yet another beautiful trait of the perfect servant comes before us in the scenes that follow. Though this blessed One has all authority and power He is *accessible to all.* When He enters the humble home of a fisherman, and there is one in need of His healing power, we read, *"Anon they tell Him of her."* Again, when the sun was set, *"they brought unto Him* all that were diseased." With the great men of this world it is far otherwise. The greater their authority and power the less accessible they are to the poor and needy. Nor is the Lord any different to-day: though high in heavenly glory we can "tell Him", and bring "unto Him", all our sorrows and our needs.

Not only did He heal men of divers diseases, He also delivered them from the power of demons. But while manifesting His complete power over demons, He "suffered not the demons to speak because they knew Him". As one has said, "He refused a testimony that was not of God. It might be true, but He would not accept the testimony of the enemy."

VERSE 35

The crowded scene of the busy evening is followed by an early morning scene when, a great while before day, we are permitted to see the Lord departing into a solitary place to pray. Thus we learn that *dependence upon God,* expressed by prayer, is another mark of the perfect Servant. The power of service in public is found in prayer in secret. We hear the voice of Jesus, through the prophet, anticipating this moment, as He says, "The Lord God hath given me the tongue of the instructed, that I should know how to speak a word in season to him that is weary: He wakeneth morning by morning, He wakeneth mine ear to hear as the instructed" (Isaiah 50:4). We have seen the Lord using the tongue of the instructed; now we see Him with the opened ear, to hear as the instructed. Thus we learn that prayer is behind His teaching (21), and His preaching (39). Well for us to seek to follow His perfect example and begin our day with God in prayer, before we face our fellow men in public, for it is difficult to find a "solitary place" in the burden and heat of the day.

VERSES 36-39

The disciples follow, and having found the Lord, they say, "All men seek for Thee." This brings to light another mark of the perfect Servant — *the refusal of mere popularity*. Nature might argue that if all are seeking us, it is the time to stay: but that was the moment when the Lord said, "Let us go into the next town." As the Servant of Jehovah He was not here to win popularity, but to do the will of God.

VERSES 40-42

We have seen the power of the servant, and the secret of power; now we are permitted to see *the grace* that makes the power available for the vilest of sinners. A poor leper, driven by his need and attracted by a power which he realises can meet his need, comes to the Lord, but with a doubt as to His grace to use the power on behalf of one whose loathsome disease made him an outcast from man. Thus, he says, "If Thou *wilt*, Thou canst make me clean." Looking at Christ he had no doubt as to His power; looking at himself he questioned the Lord's grace. So, at times, with ourselves, if we get a view of the blackness of our hearts, we may question the grace of His heart, until, in His presence we find, like the leper, that the heart of Jesus is "moved with compassion" towards the vilest of sinners that turns to Him. Even so, the woman at the well, and the thief on the cross, found in Jesus One that knew the worst about them and yet had grace in His heart for them.

His grace is greater than our sin. In the case of the leper, the Lord dispels the doubt by His words, "I will", expressing the love and compassion of a heart that is ready to use His power on behalf of a needy man.

VERSES 43-45

Another beautiful trait of the perfect Servant is seen in what follows. *He does not seek His own glory*, but the glory of the One He serves. So hear the Lord saying to the healed leper, "See thou say nothing to any man." Nevertheless, he is to tell the priest and thus the law becomes a witness to the presence of God in grace. Under the law, God alone could heal the leper, and the priest could only bear witness to what God had done.

Thus, at the outset of the Lord's path of lowly service, there passes before us His perfection as the Servant. His service is marked by authority, accompanied with power. His power is combined with accessibility to the lowly and the needy, and exercised in dependence upon God: he refuses to use His power to gain popularity; it is combined with tender compassion, and never used simply to exalt Himself.

3.
The Ministry of the Lord

In the previous portion of the Gospel we have seen the perfect Servant; in this fresh division there passes before us the perfection of His service, the faith that profits by it, and the opposition that it raises. We are privileged to see that the Lord's ministry is marked by righteousness and grace — righteousness, that raises the question of sins (1-12), and grace that blesses sinners (13-17). Such a ministry at once arouses the opposition of men, for righteousness that raises the question of sins disturbs the conscience, and grace that blesses the sinner is offensive to religious pride.

VERSES 1-2

Already we have seen the Lord and His disciples at Capernaum. Now again he enters this favoured town and crowds assemble to whom the Lord preached the word. It looked, indeed, as if souls were eager to hear the truth; but, alas! a little later the Lord has to say, "Thou Capernaum which art exalted unto heaven, shall be brought down to hell, for if the mighty works which have been done in thee, had been done in Sodom it would have remained until this day. But, I say unto you it shall be more tolerable for the land of Sodom in the day of judgment than for thee." It was at Capernaum the man was delivered from the unclean spirit; there Simon's wife's mother was healed; there it was that all the diseased were brought to Him in crowds, and were healed, and there the sick of the palsy received the forgiveness of his sins. Capernaum was, indeed, brought near to heaven, and the power and grace of heaven, but all in vain, as far as the mass were concerned. As in that day, so in this, mere crowds do not mean that souls are exercised or consciences are awakened. The advent of the Lord in their midst was but a nine days wonder in their eyes; but, before God, the lack of repentance in the presence of such a ministry left them in a more terrible plight.

VERSES 3-4

Nevertheless, where there was faith in Christ there the blessing was received. God's work is not done by mass movements, but by individual work in souls, and where there is faith there will be difficulties to overcome. The palsied man was in himself helpless, so was "borne of four"; but, even so "they could not come nigh unto Him for the press". But faith overcomes every obstacle.

VERSE 5

The Lord recognises their faith, and, as ever in His dealings with us, looks beyond the mere outward need that may bring us to Himself and deals first with the root of the trouble. Beyond the disease of the palsied man, as of all disease, there is the question of sin that has brought disease and death into the world. It may be that the man, and those who brought him, were little exercised as to the sins, nevertheless they had faith in the Lord and at once the Lord responds to this faith and can begin to unfold the blessings of those that believe; thus, He can say "Thy sins be forgiven thee."

VERSES 6-7

The moment the Lord uses His power to forgive sins the opposition commences. Men did not object to demons being cast out and diseases being healed, and lepers being cleansed, for these things relieved man of bodily trials without necessarily disturbing his conscience. Directly He speaks of sins, the conscience is touched, and men begin to oppose. They say, "Who can forgive sins but God only?" Their argument was true in principle, for God alone can forgive sins: it was wrong in application, for they failed to see the glory of the Person who was present — God manifest in flesh.

VERSE 8

The reasoners are left without excuse for the Lord proceeds to give evidence of the glory of His Person. He shows that they are in the presence of One from Whom no thoughts are hidden. They may have uttered no word, but all was known to the Searcher of hearts, Who can say, "Why reason ye these things *in your hearts*?" Is not the answer to their reasonings, as to all human reasonings, that where there is no sense of need there is no realization of the glory of the Person of Christ?

VERSES 9-12

In grace the Lord speaks another word which manifests His divine power in a way that even nature can appreciate. Whether is it easier to say "Thy sins be forgiven thee; or to say, Arise, and take up thy bed, and walk?" It has been truly said, "They were equally easy to God, alike impossible to man." In order that men "may know" that the Lord had power to forgive, He also said to the palsied man "Arise, and take up thy bed, and go thy way into thine house." This outward sign of power guaranteed the inward gift of grace. The people at once say, "We never saw it on this fashion."

VERSES 13-15

The proclamation of the forgiveness of sins has aroused the resentment of the Jewish leaders. This opposition is the first sign of the total rejection of Christ which involved the setting aside of the Jews. Hence it becomes the occasion of bringing to light, in the call of Levi, an intimation of the new dispensation about to be introduced by the Lord. Thus we read, "He went forth by *the sea side.*" The sea in Scripture is often used to set forth nations, and therefore is suggestive of the great truth that the Lord was about to become the gathering centre of Christianity for believers from Jews and Gentiles. The word to Levi was, "Follow Me." Moreover, the fact that Levi was a publican, or taxgatherer, sets forth the great characteristic of Christianity in contrast to the law. No occupation was more degraded and scandalous in the eyes of a Jew, than that of a man who made his living by the extortion of tribute for the hated Roman. That the Lord should call such was great grace that lifts a man from the lowest place of degradation as a sinner into the highest place in the service of the Lord as an apostle. At once Levi responds to the call, and makes a feast in his house to which he invites many publicans and sinners to meet the Saviour of sinners.

VERSE 16

Such a display of grace stirs up the opposition of those marked by the pride of intellect and the pride of religion. They were deeply offended by the grace that, passing them by, takes a sinner, far beneath them in moral degradation, and lifts him into a place far above them in blessing and power. These opposers do not approach Christ, as an exercised soul would have done, but they turn to the disciples, and, as the Serpent tried to shake the woman's confidence in God by asking what appeared to be a very simple question, so these men attempt to shake the confidence of the disciples in the Lord by asking what might appear to them a very reasonable question, "How is it that He eateth and drinketh with publicans and sinners?"

VERSE 17

The Lord disposes of this question with a simple illustration, 'They that are whole have no need of the physician, but they that are sick." He then applies the illustration, by saying, "I came not to call the righteous, but sinners." They insinuated that the Lord was associating with sinners; His reply is that He was "calling" sinners out of their things to follow Him. Grace to the sinner does not mean indifference to his sins.

VERSE 18

But the Pharisees grow more bold. They had sought to undermine confidence in the Lord by going to the disciples with questions about the Lord; now they will seek to find fault with the disciples by raising questions with the Lord about the disciples. "Why do the disciples of John and of the Pharisees fast, but thy disciples fast not?"

VERSES 19-22

Again the Lord uses an illustration to expose their folly. Would it be seemly to fast in the presence of the Bridegroom? In like manner would it be appropriate to fast in the presence of the One Who was dispensing blessing on every hand? The days were coming when Christ would be no longer present. Solemn consideration for these opposers of grace; then, indeed, fasting would be appropriate; not simply fasting from food, but from the pleasures of a world that has rejected Christ. As ever, the Lord does more than answer their question. He proves that their question exposes their utter incapacity to enter into the new ways of God in grace. The new character of grace displayed in life and walk and ways, could not be attached to the older order any more than a piece of new cloth could be attached to an old garment. Nor can the inner life, and power of this new life, be contained in the old vessels. New wine demands new vessels. The power and energy of the Holy Spirit cannot have anything to say to the flesh. The Lord was introducing that which was entirely new, set forth in figure by the "new cloth", the "new wine", and the "new bottles". When the new is brought in we cannot go back to the old. Alas! Christendom has attempted to do so by attaching the forms of Judaism to Christianity. The doctrines of grace have been acknowledged, while in practice the forms of the law have been adopted.

VERSES 23-29

In the incident that took place on the Sabbath, we see a further intimation that the whole system, represented by the Sabbath, was about to be set aside. In raising the question of the Sabbath, the Pharisees profess great zeal for the outward observance of a day, while wholly indifferent to the fact that the Lord of the Sabbath, and His disciples were left to hunger. They assumed to be glorifying God at the very moment when they were rejecting His witness. The Lord exposes their unreality by recalling the history of David and his companions, who in the day of their rejection were left to hunger. In these circumstances, when God's anointed was rejected, and hunted, and hungered, the shewbread ceases to have its value in His sight, and therefore no sin was committed though David and

THE GOSPEL OF MARK

his companions acted contrary to the letter of the law in eating of the shewbread. So with the Sabbath: it was for the blessing of men, and not for increasing the sufferings of hungry men. Moreover, "The Son of Man is Lord also of the sabbath", and therefore above the Sabbath that He instituted.

Thus in the course of the chapter we are permitted to see *the righteousness* that raises the question of sins; *the grace* that forgives sins and calls sinners, and *the faith* that obtains the blessing. Then we see the opposition that the natural heart, if left to itself, will ever raise against a ministry of righteousness and grace. Lastly, this position becomes the occasion of showing the change in the dispensation about to take place.

4.
The Change of Dispensation

CHAPTER 3

In the former chapters we have seen the perfect Servant, in His ministry of grace and power, dispensing blessing in the midst of the Jewish nation. We have also seen that, while this ministry brought to light the faith of a godly remnant, it also aroused the enmity of the leaders of the nation who dared to charge the Lord with being a blasphemer, of associating with sinners and breaking the sabbath.

This opposition foreshadowed the great change of dispensation about to take place. The Jews, who reject their Messiah and commit the unpardonable sin against the Holy Ghost, will be set aside and grace will flow out to the Gentiles. The old order, under law in Judaism, will give place to the reign of grace under Christianity. This change of dispensation is indicated, in this fresh division of the Gospel, by a series of incidents that take place in the synagogue (1-6); by the sea (7-12); on the mountain (13-19); and in an house (19-35). Each place and scene has its special significance.

Verses 1-6

The first incident tells us that the Lord "again entered into the synagogue", thus setting forth His presence in the midst of the Jewish nation — for the synagogue was the meeting place of those under law. What an arresting scene takes place in this synagogue at Capernaum! God's perfect Servant — the Lord of glory — is present with power to bless, and grace in His heart to use the power on behalf of the needy. Man is there in all his deep need, but powerless to help himself, for his hand is withered. The religious man is there with no sense of his need, no realisation of the glory of the Lord, and indifferent to the need of others.

Of these Pharisees, we read that "they watched Him", not to learn of His ways and the grace of His heart, but in the hope that He would do good "on the sabbath day" in the healing of a poor needy man that was present, and thus give them occasion to bring a charge against the Lord of working on the sabbath. What a witness to the perfection of Christ, that His enemies do not expect any evil from Him, but can count upon His doing good! And in our day, and measure, do not the men of the world bear unconscious witness to the truth of Christianity, inasmuch as they expect Christians to do good and act in a way different to themselves. If Christianity is all false, why should unbelievers expect the Christians to act in a better way than themselves?

If the Lord was not the Son of God and the Servant of Jehovah, why should these Jews expect Him to heal this man? They unconsciously bear witness to the grace of His heart and the hardness of their own hearts. Seeing that the Lord knew what was in their hearts and that they were seeking an occasion against Him, we might judge it would have been prudent to refrain from healing the man in public, and thus deprive these wicked men of the opportunity that they sought. But the Lord was here to manifest the grace of God and so proceeds to act with the utmost publicity. He tells the man to "stand forth" before them all. By His question the Lord gives these men an opportunity to state their difficulties as to healing on the sabbath day. But we read, "They held their peace." This silence was not that lowly grace that marked the Lord when, in the presence of insults, He answered never a word. It was the silence of mere policy and, more eloquently than words, exposed the impotent hatred of their hearts. The Lord looked upon them with righteous anger. But behind the anger there was distress. He was grieved for the hardness of their hearts that was wholly indifferent to the need of the man, perfectly helpless to meet that need, and bitterly opposed to the One who had both the grace and the power to bless. In result, the men that would not allow the Lord to do good on the sabbath, were perfectly prepared to do evil. Already they had watched to accuse Him; now they take counsel to destroy the Blesser.

VERSES 7-12

The malice of the Jew cannot stay the grace of the Lord, or check His unwearied service of love. It does, indeed, divert that service into other channels, and become the occasion of grace reaching a wider circle. This change in the ways of God is suggested by the Lord withdrawing from the synagogue — the Jewish centre — and taking His place by the sea, so often used in Scripture as a figure of the nations. The rejection of Christ by the Jew opens the door for the blessing of the Gentile.

Further, in this new position, we have an indication of the new principles which mark the day of grace. The Jews in the synagogue were governed by sight — "they watched Him"; their hearts were hardened to their own need, and filled with enmity to the One who alone could meet their need. In contrast, by the sea side, "a great multitude", including Gentiles, were attracted to the Lord "when they had *heard* what great things He did". Faith cometh by hearing and is the outcome of a sense of need. For, if they were drawn to Christ by His grace, they were driven to Him by their need. "As many as *had plagues*" came. Solomon, in his prayer, speaks of every man knowing "the plague of his own heart", and points the only way of relief in spreading it out before God (1 Kings 8:38). A plague in the heart is something known only to the individual, that comes in to mar his joy. Some question between the soul and God that is unsettled; it may be some secret sin unconfessed. Faith, realising the grace that is in the heart of Christ, can spread the plague out before Him, and find deliverance from every evil influence.

Verses 13-19

Again the scene changes from the sea to the mountain. The Lord had been with the Jews in their synagogue to find only the withered hand, the hard heart, and deadly enmity. He had been by the sea side the centre of attraction for needy souls, drawn from Jews and Gentiles. Now we are lifted above man's world to learn on the mountain something of the new ways of God. In the sovereign choice of the Twelve we see the foundation laid for the new order of blessing about to be introduced. The Church is called out from Jews and Gentiles, and is "built upon the foundation of the apostles and prophets, Jesus Christ Himself being the chief corner stone" (Ephesians 2:20). When at last we have a description of the Church in glory, we find in the foundation of the city the names of the Twelve Apostles of the Lamb (Revelation 21:14).

This new work does not flow from the responsibility of man. It is wholly of God. The Lord, having separated

Himself from man and his world, according to His own sovereign choice "calleth unto Him whom He would". He calls them, He ordains them, He sends them forth, and He gives them power. But above all, they are chosen that "they should *be with Him*". The nearest and dearest object of His heart is to have His people with Himself. Here, however, it is specially in view of service, for which the only true preparation is the company of the Lord. So the Lord could say in an earlier scene, *"Come ye after me, and I will make you to become fishers of men"* (and again, at a later day, "if any man serve me, let him follow me" (John 12:26)). To reach Christ we must be separate from the world, even as He is, set forth by following Him into the mountain. There, from His company, in the separate place, they are sent forth to preach the glad tidings. This was something entirely new. In the Jewish system there was, indeed, the reading and expounding of the law in their synagogues, but there was no preaching. This new thing was to be introduced with the power to heal diseases, and cast out demons. Christ, not only does miracles Himself, but, He can give others the power to perform them.

VERSES 19-21

Associating the disciples with Himself, the Lord now enters into an house. Connected with the house we have the relations of the Lord according to the flesh. If in the mountain we see the foundation laid for that which is entirely new, in the house we learn that the Lord no longer owns any connection with Israel after the flesh. His relatives felt the reproach of being connected with One who was condemned by their leaders, and whose teaching and practice condemned the world. Not being prepared for the reproach of Christ, they would seek to restrain Him, for they said, "He is out of His mind." They probably admitted all the hard things that their leaders said about Him, but they said, "He is beside himself", and should be put under restraint.

Verse 22

The scribes from Jerusalem, who by reason of their official position and intellectual superiority, had power and influence with the people, will not accept the plea of madness. They knew it was not the diseased mind of a madman, concentrating all his energy on one aim, but a very real power that cast out demons. They knew it was a power above that of man. They would not own it was of God, and hence they were compelled to impute His power to the devil — the only other power.

Verses 23-30

This terrible charge seals their doom. And yet with what perfect calm and grace the Lord meets this wickedness. In the mountain the Lord had just called unto Himself the Twelve, to associate them with Himself in blessing. Now He calls His enemies unto Him to pronounce their doom. Solemn thought! The One who calls in grace, will call in judgment. The Lord shows that their charge was, not only ignorant folly, but deliberate blasphemy against the Holy Ghost. Here was One who was stronger than the strong man, who was taking his goods from him, showing, indeed, that He had bound the strong man. All this power was exercised by the Lord Jesus in the power of the Holy Ghost (compare Acts 10:38). Hence to ascribe His power to the devil was to call the Holy Ghost a demon. This was a sin that could not be pardoned. It was the end of all hope for Israel on the ground of responsibility. This, then, is the solemn climax to all the Lord's gracious service in this world. "Man can see nothing in the activity of divine

goodness but madness and the work of the devil"
(J.N.Darby).

VERSES *31-35*

The solemn scene that follows is the terrible result for the
Jewish nation. All relationship with Israel after the flesh is
renounced. Every link with the nation is broken. At the
same time the Lord distinguishes a remnant who are in
relationship with Himself, not by reason of their natural
connection with Israel, but by faith in His word (see John
6:39, 40).

5.
Fruit for God and Light for Man

CHAPTER 4

In the fourth chapter of Mark we have four parables, and the incident of the storm on the lake, giving a complete picture of the Lord's service on earth at His first coming, with the result of that service when left to the responsibility of men during the time of His absence.

VERSES 1-20

The rejection of Christ by the Jewish leaders, and the consequent breaking of all links with Israel according to the flesh, on the part of Christ, as set forth in chapter 3, gives occasion to reveal the true character of the Lord's service. Up to this moment, in His ministry of grace, it might appear that He was seeking fruit from Israel; it now becomes manifest, by the parable of the Sower, that, actually, He was doing a work to produce fruit. His ministry was, indeed, a test for Israel proving that there is no fruit for God from fallen man, as such. If there is to be any fruit it can only be through God's own work in the souls of men set forth in figure by the sowing of the seed.

Moreover, if a work of God is necessary, it cannot be confined to one nation. It proves that the Jew is as needy as the Gentile, and that both alike are helpless to secure their own blessing. Thus the Lord's service of grace has in view all the world. This truth may be indicated by the fact that the Lord "began again to teach by the *sea side*".

In the strict interpretation of the parable we must all recognise that the Lord is the Sower, and the seed is the word of God. Therefore the Sower was perfect, the sowing was faultless, and the seed good. Nevertheless, owing to the character of the soil, in three cases out of four no lasting result is produced. The parable indicates that when the gospel is preached, it may be listened to by four different characters of hearers. To use the language of the parable, there are "way side" hearers; "stony ground" hearers; some likened to "thorny ground", and, lastly, some "good ground" hearers.

The "way side" hearers are those who hear without the conscience being reached. It is like seed that falls on the hard road, but does not penetrate beneath the surface. The birds of the air can easily devour such seed, and Satan can take away that which is of only passing interest to the mind without touching the conscience.

The seed that falls on stony ground springs up and makes a certain amount of show, but before the heat of the sun it fades away because there is no depth of earth. The Lord explains that this represents those who, when they have heard the word, immediately receive it with gladness, but there is no work of God in their souls. It is not a good sign when a soul, without previous exercise, receives the word with joy. If God is working with a soul, He deals with the conscience, awakening a sense of sins and guilt. Thus the first effect of the word is not joy but trouble. This leads to self-judgment and repentance towards God. Following upon self-judgment the darkness passes and the light of God penetrates the dark heart producing exercise which is met by the love of God inspiring confidence, when the light has done its work.

The third case is that of one who hears the good news, but the word is choked and produces no lasting result. In each case the Lord is speaking of those who have *heard* the word, not of those who have never heard the gospel. Hearing the word would denote some kind of profession that would lead to the hope that there is true conversion until proved to be otherwise. The thorny ground hearers represent those who are so overwhelmed by anxiety as to present things, or so active in the pursuit of worldly things, that their profession fades away. The lust of other things chokes the one thing needful. The poor may be crushed by cares; the rich by the deceitfulness of riches. How solemn for the soul to be ruined by cares or lost by riches! What shall it profit a man if he gain the whole world and lose his own soul?

The last case is the good ground hearer. Good ground is always prepared ground. The conscience has been reached, and as a result fruit is produced, but, even so, it is in different degrees, some thirty, some sixty, and some an hundredfold. The things which are fatal to the unbeliever may grievously hinder the fruitfulness of the true believer.

Verse 21

In the second parable we learn that the one who has received the good seed of the word into the heart is fitted, and responsible, to be a witness before men. That which is fruit for God becomes light to man. The shining of the light is not a question of gift, nor the exercise of gift in preaching and teaching, but rather the new life expressing something of Christ as being like Christ, "blameless and harmless, the sons of God, without rebuke, in the midst of a crooked and perverse generation among whom ye shine as lights in the world" (Philippians 2:15).

The Lord warns us that, as there are hindrances to the seed becoming effectual, so, when the word has truly wrought in the heart, there may be hindrances to the light shining out to others. Even as the seed may be choked by the cares of this world, or the deceitfulness of riches, so the light may be dimmed, on the one hand, by our lives being absorbed in the business of life, represented by the bushel; or, on the other hand, by seeking to take our ease, as set forth by the bed. The Christian is viewed not as the light, but as the light-holder. Christ is the light, the Christian is the candlestick, or light-bearer.

VERSE 22

How far we have been faithful, or unfaithful, in bearing witness for Christ, will at last be made manifest. The secret for shining for Christ is having Christ in the heart. "Unless the heart be full of Christ, the truth will not be manifested: if the heart be full of other things, of itself, Christ cannot be manifested" (J.N.Darby).

VERSE 23

How then are our hearts to be filled with Christ? The Lord's exhortation indicates that if we are to enlighten others we must first hear for ourselves, "If any man have ears to hear, *let him hear.*" The Lord Himself, can say through the prophet, "The Lord, Jehovah, hath given me the tongue of the instructed, that I should know how to succour by a word him that is weary. He wakeneth morning by morning, He wakeneth mine ear *to hear as the instructed*" (Isaiah 50:4 N.Tr.). If we are to have the tongue of the instructed, we must first have the ear of the learner. If we are to know how to succour by a word him that is weary, we must first hear the word of One who is never weary. Like Mary of old, we must sit at His feet, to hear His word, before we can witness to others.

VERSES 24-25

Moreover, in witnessing to others we ourselves shall be blessed, for the Lord can say, "With what measure ye mete, it shall be measured to you." The more we give to others, the more will be given to us. If the light we have is allowed to shine, we shall get more light. One has truly said that Heaven's law is 'Scattering for increase'. But let us also remember that if we do not use the light we have we shall lose it. It is not life, but light, that we lose.

VERSES 26-29

The Lord uses a third parable to show that the time in which the believer's testimony is rendered, is during His absence. The Kingdom of God was about to take the form in which the King would be absent. It is as if a man, having cast the seed into the ground, does nothing further until the time of the harvest. The Lord had personally sown the seed at His first coming, and at the end of the age will personally return when the judgment of this world is ripe. Between His first and second coming the Lord is at the right hand of God, and though ever working in grace, on behalf of His people, He does not publicly and directly interfere in the affairs of this world. The seed, however, that the Lord has sown grows and brings forth fruit.

VERSES 30-34

The last parable sets forth the result of the seed-sowing when left to the responsibility of man. Christianity, which in its beginning was very small in man's sight, even like a "grain of mustard seed", becomes in the hands of man a great power on the earth. But in its greatness, it becomes a shelter for evil. "The fowls of the air lodge under the shelter of it." That which at the beginning gathered souls out of this world around the Lord, in the end becomes a vast system which shelters every evil thing.

Verses 35-41

The incident of the storm on the lake, presents a picture that completes the teaching of the chapter. We have seen the Lord sowing the good seed, and then learnt that those in whose hearts the seed has become effectual, are left in this world to be a light for Christ. By the third parable we have been instructed that this witness would take place during the absence of Christ. In the last parable we learn that, during His absence, there would grow up a vast religious profession that would become a shelter for evil. Now we learn that, in such a world, the Lord's true people will meet with trials, but that the Lord Jesus, though absent to sight, is present to faith, and is supreme over all the storms His people have to meet.

The touching scene is opened with the Lord's words, "Let us pass over unto the other side." His last words to Peter, ere He left this world were, "Follow thou Me." Attracted to Himself by our need, and drawn by His grace, we follow Him in a path that leads to "the other side" — far into those depths of glory where He has gone. If, however, we are in company *with Him*, we may expect conflict, for the devil is ever opposed to Christ. Thus, in the picture, we read, "there arose a great storm of wind". Nevertheless, Jesus was with them, but He was "asleep on a pillow". As in the parable, having sown the seed, He was as one that slept (verse 27), so actually in the storm He was asleep, and thus apparently indifferent to the trials of His people. Such circumstances become a very real test to our faith,

THE GOSPEL OF MARK

and, like the disciples, we may even begin to question whether, after all, He cares for us. But if such circumstances are allowed to prove our faith, they also become the occasion of manifesting His supremacy over all the trials we have to meet. As of old, He "arose and rebuked the wind, and said unto the sea, Peace, be still", so today, in His own time and way, He can still every storm and bring us into "a great calm". In the spirit of this striking picture, the apostle can write to the Thessalonian believers saying, "Now the Lord of peace Himself give you peace always by all means. The Lord *be with you all*" (2 Thessalonians 3:16). Faith realises that whatever storms we may have to meet, the Lord is with us to give peace at all times and in all circumstances. Occupied with "a great storm of wind and the waves" that beat into our little ship, we may forget Christ and selfishly think only of ourselves, and then say, like the disciples, "We perish." But will any storm that the devil can raise ever frustrate the counsels of God for Christ and His people? Not one of His sheep will ever perish; all will be brought home at last. The trouble with the disciples, as too often with ourselves, is that we have but a feeble sense of the glory of the Person that is with us. They but little realised that the Man that was with them was also the Son of God.

6.
The Individual Blessing of Souls

CHAPTER 5

We have seen the perfect Servant sowing the good seed. Now we are permitted to see another form of His service — the dealing with individual souls. In this gracious service we see, not only the spiritual blessing of souls, but also divine power overcoming the devil, disease, and death. It thus becomes clear that, in the Person of the Lord, God was present with grace and power to deliver man from the effects of sin; but, even so, man finds the presence of God intolerable.

VERSES 1-5

In the story of the demoniac we have first brought vividly before us the utter misery of the man *under the power of Satan*. We see a man "who had his dwelling among the tombs". Where men dwell, there they die, and hard by their dwellings will ever be found a burying place with its tombs, ever reminding us that this world is under the shadow of death. All Satan's power is put forth to drive men into death. "The thief cometh not but for to steal, and to kill and to destroy" (John 10:10). He would rob us of every spiritual blessing, kill the body, and destroy the soul.

Secondly, the story shows the utter *helplessness* of man to deliver himself, or others, from the power of Satan. All the efforts to restrain the violence of this poor man, or to tame him were in vain. So today every attempt to restrain evil or reform the flesh entirely fails to deliver the world from its violence and corruption, from the power of Satan, or to change the flesh.

Verses 6-13

Thirdly, we learn that though we are ruined and helpless, yet, in the Person of Christ there is One with power and grace to deliver us from all the power of Satan. The poor man is so entirely identified with the unclean spirit that his body is the dwelling place and instrument of the demon, who acts and speaks through the man. But demons have to bow in the presence of One that they know is the Son of God with all power to consign them to their just doom. Men may be ignorant of the glory and authority of Christ, but not so demons. Seeing that at the word of Christ they must come out of the man, they ask that they may be sent into swine. Apparently evil spirits require some natural body through which to act. Having obtained leave, they enter the swine with the result that the destructive malice of the demons is at once seen for in their case there was no restraint that the demons could not at once overcome. Thus the whole herd immediately rushes to destruction.

Verses 14-17

Fourthly we learn from this solemn incident that if the power of Satan is terrible to man, the presence of God is intolerable, even when present in power and grace to deliver man. One has said man is "more afraid of Jesus and His grace than of the devil and his works." The men of the city, coming out "to see what it was that was done" are at once faced with the evidence of the grace and power of Jesus. The man who had long been a trial to the country, they find "sitting, and clothed, and in his right mind". Beautiful picture of a truly converted soul, delivered from the terrible power of Satan, and brought to rest at the feet of Jesus; no longer naked and exposed to judgment, but clothed, cleared from every charge, justified before God, Christ his righteousness, and in his right mind — reconciled, with all the enmity against God withered up.

Then we read, "They were afraid." What a comment upon the men of this world! They see the evidence that God had drawn very near, and they were afraid. Guilty man is ever afraid of God. Adam, fallen, was afraid; Israel, at Sinai, were afraid, and the men of Gadara were afraid. It matters not how God comes, whether as a visitor in the Garden of Eden, in majesty at Sinai, or in grace as at Gadara, the presence of God is insupportable to guilty man. Men prefer the demons, the demoniac, and the swine, rather than the Son of God even though He be present in power and grace to deliver man. So we read "They began to pray Him to depart out of their coasts." Their prayer was answered — He departed.

Verses 18-20

Lastly, we see, in striking contrast to the men of this world, that the man that has been so richly blessed desires to be *with Jesus*. In due time his desire will have a glorious answer, for we know that Christ had died for believers that "we should live together with Him", and very soon we shall be for ever with the Lord. In the meantime we have the privilege of being *for Him* in a scene from which He has been rejected. Thus the Lord can say to the man, "Go home to thy friends, and tell them how great things the Lord hath done for thee, and hath had compassion on thee." And what was the result? "All men did marvel." The more we realise our utter ruin under the power of Satan and what Christ has done for us, and the compassion shown toward us, the more we may marvel.

VERSES 21-23

Underlying the incidents of this chapter there is surely dispensational teaching setting forth the ways of God with Israel and the nations. From the herd driven into the sea, are we not intended to learn that, as the result of the rejection of their Messiah, the Jews were about to be scattered among the sea of nations? In the incident that follows the dying child, do we not see a picture of the condition of the nation morally when the Lord was present? But even as in the end of the story the Lord raised the child from death, so, when He returns to earth He will revive the nation. In the meantime we learn, from the story of the woman, that wherever there are individuals that have faith in Christ they will obtain the blessing.

VERSE 24

In the case of the woman the Lord distinguishes between true faith and mere outward profession. Seeing that "much people followed Him and thronged Him", it might appear that the Lord was surrounded by a number of believing followers. Even so today it might seem as we see religious buildings crowded with professed worshippers of Christ, as we hear the Name of Christ taken upon the lips of men and women of the world in hymns and prayers, and as we hear the Name of Christ attached to the works of men, that there are a vast host of believers in Christ. Indeed, men do so judge, for they speak of themselves as Christians, call their lands Christian countries, and speak of their governments as Christian governments. But does this imply that all are true believers in the Lord Jesus? That all have personal faith in Christ? Alas, no! There is still the great throng of outward profession; and still the Lord distinguishes those who have personal faith in Himself, for we read, "The Lord knoweth them that are His." The crowd may have been sincere, for they saw the miracles and enjoyed the benefits that they received from Christ, but with no sense of their need of Christ they had no personal faith in Christ. Even so today, people may be quite sincere when they adopt, as they say, the Christian religion. But this outward profession of Christianity — this joining the throng to follow Jesus — will not save the soul, will not settle the question of sins, and death and judgment: will not break the power of sin, or deliver from the corruptions of the flesh and the world and the fear of death.

Verse 25

For true blessing there must be personal faith in the Lord Jesus. In the case of the woman we have this personal touch of faith very blessedly illustrated. First we see that where there is faith there will always be some sense of need of a personal Saviour. The sense of need may vary greatly in different cases, but it will be there.

Verse 26

Secondly, not only was she conscious of her need, but she realised the utter hopelessness of her case as far as her own efforts, and the skill of man, were concerned. She had suffered many things of many physicians and had spent all in vain attempts to meet her need.

Verses 27-29

Thirdly, faith is not only conscious of need, and our own helplessness to meet the need, but perceives something of the excellency of the Person of Jesus — sees, indeed, that in Him there is grace and power to meet the need. Moreover faith makes a person humble. The needy soul is ready to take the lowly place and to say, like the woman, "If I may but touch the hem of His garment, I shall be whole." We have not to do some great thing to secure the blessing, that would only pander to our pride, but we are made willing to be nothing and to give Christ all the glory. The virtue is in Christ, not in the faith; the touch of faith secures the blessing by putting us in touch with the One in Whom is all the merit.

VERSES 30-34

Then we see that the Lord delights to encourage faith. He is not content that the one who has received the blessing should go quietly away. He brings the believer into His own presence there to tell him all the truth. He delights that we should have everything out with Him — that there should be no distance or reserve between Himself and His own.

Lastly, we see the result of getting into the presence of the Lord and having all out with Him. Like the woman we can then go on our way, not trusting in our feelings or in some experience, however real, but with the assurance of His own word. Thus the woman learns from His own lips that she was healed, for He can say, "Thy faith hath made thee whole."

VERSES 35-43

While the Lord is dealing with the case of the woman, there comes one from the house of the ruler, saying, "Thy daughter is dead: why troublest thou the Master any further?" This person little knew either the power of His hand or the tender love of His heart. However deep our sorrows, however great our trials, we need not fear to "trouble" the Lord with our burdens. He was here to share our griefs and bear our trials. Entering into the feelings of the poor father, the Lord drops a word of comfort into his heart — "Be not afraid, only believe." As far as man was concerned the case was manifestly hopeless, the child was dead. But the case was not beyond the reach of Christ. Having dealt with unbelief and put out those who laughed Him to scorn He raised the child and cared for her needs.

7.
The Service of Christ
when Rejected

CHAPTER 6

The great truths that come before us in chapter six are connected with incidents that take place in the country, the king's court, the desert place, the mountain and the stormy sea. In the first two incidents we learn the low moral condition of the world that rejects Christ: in the last three, we discover the fulness of the resources in Christ for those who follow Him apart from the course of this world.

VERSES 1-6

In the first scene we see the Lord in His lowly service of love associating with the humble folk of "His own country", "His own kin", and "His own house". He comes into their midst with divine wisdom, and divine power, ministering the truth among the poor of the land, and healing some sick folk; but in no wise does He pander to the vanity of human nature that loves pomp and display, and rejects men because of their humble origin. The Lord's ministry of grace makes manifest this low moral condition of the people. They are indeed astounded at His teaching and His wisdom, and cannot but admit His "mighty works", but "they were offended at Him". The flesh is ever the same, so that in our day are we not in danger, at times, even as Christians, of hindering the work of God by the pride and vanity of the flesh that slights the ministry of a servant of God because of his humble origin; or, as servants, we may fail by seeking to obtain a hearing on the ground of wealth or social position. With the Lord all was perfect; the failure was on the part of the people. These simple country folk belittled the wisdom of the Lord's teaching, and the might of His works by saying, "Is not this the carpenter, the son of Mary?" And they said, "His brothers and sisters are with us." They failed to discern the glory of His Person and the grace of His heart, that though He was rich yet for our sakes He had become poor that we through His poverty might be made rich. Thus the Creator had become the Carpenter, and the Son of God the Son of Mary. The Lord reminds those that reject Him, because of His humiliation, that "A prophet is not without honour, but in his own country, and amongst his own kin, and in his own house." This does not imply that the Lord was rejected in His own country, as we might be, because of known weakness or failure, but that familiarity with Him in the affairs of this life are used to discount His divine mission from God.

The result is He could there do no mighty work because of their unbelief. It is a solemn consideration how much, in our day, unbelief may hinder the work of God. If faith, as in the case of the sick woman of the last chapter, draws forth the blessing, it is equally true that unbelief hinders its outflow. Nevertheless, His grace, rising above our pride and unbelief, healed some "sick folk" even though the blessing is limited to "a few". "He marvelled because of their unbelief." Alas! do we not at times give Him occasion to marvel at our unbelief? Nevertheless He pursued His way, teaching in the villages round about, unwearied in His service in spite of pride and unbelief.

VERSES 7-13

The rejection of His service may hinder any performance of a mighty work in His own country, but it cannot stay the grace of His heart. Thus the Lord sends forth the twelve as a fresh witness to His presence in grace and power for the blessing of men. A striking witness is borne to His glory as a Divine Person by the fact that He "gave them power over unclean spirits". Anyone can exercise power and perform miracles if the power is given to them; but, who but God can *give the power*? Further the manner in which they went forth was, in itself, a witness to the presence of the Lord of all. They were to go forth taking nothing for their journey. They were to rest in the providing care and protection of the Lord present on earth, who would so dispose of the hearts of men, and govern circumstances, that they would lack nothing.

Their mission was not to degenerate into a social round of visits. They were on the service of the Lord, and therefore were to abide in the same house in any particular place. The substance of their preaching was repentance, for the presence of the King, and the good news of the Kingdom, had been proclaimed, with the result that the leaders had rejected Christ because of the greatness of His claims, while the people had refused Him because of the lowliness of His position. The leaders accused Him of doing His mighty works by the power of the devil; the people said He is only a carpenter. The nation is called to repent of this wickedness. Moreover, it was a final testimony for judgment was to be pronounced upon those that rejected this mission.

VERSES *14-29*

The result of this mission, accompanied by signs of power, was that "His name was spread abroad". Would that all servants so ministered Christ that they left behind them a savour of Christ, and the sense of the preciousness of His Name. Alas! too often the preacher may be so advertised, and so many methods adopted that appeal to the natural man, that the preacher's name becomes spread abroad rather than the Name of Jesus

Nevertheless, however widely the fame of Jesus may be proclaimed, unless there is a work of God in the soul, it only leads to speculation, as in that day, when some said that it was John the Baptist risen from the dead, others that it was a prophet. But the speculations of the human mind never reach the truth as to the Person of Christ. However, the fame of Christ reaches the court circle. Already we have seen the utter lack of all spiritual discernment in the lower classes, now we are to learn the low moral condition of the higher circles. With king Herod, the report of Christ does more than lead to speculation, it awakens an uneasy conscience. This leads to the story of his sin. He had formed a guilty marriage with his brother's wife and had been rebuked for his sin by John the Baptist. This rebuke had aroused the enmity of Herodias the guilty adulteress. She would have killed John but could find no way to do so, for Herod feared John knowing that he was a just man and a holy. Herod, though an unprincipled man, could appreciate goodness in others, and indeed listened to John and did many things by his counsel. However, Herodias waits her time, and a court revel gave her the opportunity she sought. The king, pleased by a dance, makes a rash promise, and rather than break his promise has John killed. It has been well said, "The devil's promises are better broken than kept."

The rejection and murder of the Forerunner is a solemn indication that, in due time, Herod will take his part in the rejection and crucifixion of Christ.

VERSES 30-44

The apostles, having fulfilled their mission, "gathered themselves unto Jesus". Having been sent forth by the Lord, they now return to Him. How good for every servant, when any little service has been accomplished, to get back to the Lord and tell Him all things that they have done and taught. Too often we are inclined to tell others, though at times it may be right to encourage the Lord's people by telling them of His work. There is, however, this great difference, if we gather the assembly of God's people together, as was the case with Paul and Barnabas at Antioch, it should be to rehearse "all that *God had done, and how He had opened the door*" (Acts 14:27). But when, after service, we gather together unto Jesus, it is to tell Him what *we have done and taught*. How good for our souls to pass in review our acts and words in the presence of One, Who will never flatter, and before Whom we cannot boast, and from Whom nothing can be hid; there to learn, it may be, our weaknesses and defects. Alas! we may be full of ourselves and our service; but, in the Lord's presence we can speak freely of all that possesses the thoughts and burdens the mind, and thus have our spirits calmed so that we may think soberly of ourselves, or forget ourselves and our service to be occupied with Himself. We have no record of any comment on their service, but we learn the Lord's sympathy and care for His servants. They had spoken of their service, but He is concerned about *them* and the rest they need. Hence, He can say, "Come ye yourselves apart into a desert place and rest a while." The eternal rest remains, but here there is the "rest a while".

It has been pointed out that there are three reasons for the disciples being led apart into the desert place. First, the Lord retired into the desert on account of the murder of His witness, a sure sign of His own rejection and crucifixion. This indicated that the dispensation was about to change, and so the Lord takes a place outside and apart from the guilty nation. This dispensational reason is prominent in Matthew 14:13. Secondly, there is a reason for the Lord taking an outside place in connection with the service of His disciples. Very naturally this has a prominent place in the gospel of Mark. Their service had taken them into the world, and had created such a stir that "there were many coming and going". Under such circumstances the servant needs to be drawn apart from the restless spirit of the world to be with Himself, and rest a while. The third reason for this incident is presented in the gospel of Luke, where we learn that the disciples are drawn apart to be instructed of the Lord (Luke 9:10, 18-27).

In our day we, too, need to be withdrawn from the world to learn that we are not of it, even if sent into it on the Lord's service. Our blessings are heavenly not earthly. So, too, we need to be alone with the Lord to escape the spirit of the world, with all its restless activity, and never more so than when some little testimony for Christ has for the moment made some stir in the world. We also need to be in the privacy of the Lord's presence to learn His mind.

At the Lord's word they depart into the desert place privately. However, "the people saw them departing", and, in their eagerness to reach Christ, "outwent them, and came together unto Him." It seemed then that, after all, they would be robbed of their rest. But the Lord, in His tender care for His own, and compassion for the people, came out from the place of retirement to meet the people.

There might be rest for His disciples: there was no rest for Him. His compassion would not let Him rest; so we read, "He began to teach them many things."

When the day was far spent the disciples came from their rest, and said to the Lord, "Send them away." It would seem as if the disciples looked upon them as intruders upon their rest and would fain be rid of them. But the Lord will not send them away hungry, for is it not written, "I will satisfy her poor with bread." No failure on the part of Israel can wither up the kindness and compassion of the heart of Jehovah. He will "teach them many things" for the blessing of their souls, and provide the loaves and fishes to meet the need of their bodies. He is the same today; in spite of all our weaknesses and many failures He cares for our souls and provides for our bodies. Moreover, in carrying out this work of love, He uses others. He can say to the disciples, "Give ye them to eat." But, as so often with ourselves, their faith was not able to use His power. They can only think of how much they would require, forgetting the vast resources they had in Christ. Having made manifest the utter inadequacy of their own resources, the Lord brings their little — the five loaves and the two fishes — into touch with heaven's plenty, with the result that five thousand men "did all eat and were filled".

VERSES 45-46

The story unfolded in the following verses brings again before us the great fact that the Lord was about to leave His disciples in a world from which He was rejected. The Lord had just fed the multitude, His compassion being drawn out to them as sheep not having a Shepherd. Alas! not only were they without one to lead them into green pastures, and care for their souls, but when the Good Shepherd came into their midst they had no eyes to discern His glory and no heart to receive Him. So, the Lord having sent away the people, "departed into a mountain to pray". In picture the nation is dismissed, while He takes a new place on high to intercede for His own who are left to witness for Him in a world from which He has been rejected.

VERSES 47-52

The disciples find that not only are they bereft of the bodily presence of the Lord, but that they have to face the storms of life, and have to toil in rowing. Everything in this world is contrary to the Lord's people. But if the world is against us and the devil is opposed to us, the Lord on high is interceding for us. But if the Lord is absent, He is not indifferent to the storms and difficulties His people have to meet. "He saw them toiling", and He came to them. But He came in a way that set forth His superiority to all the circumstances they were in, for He came "walking on the water". The display of a power so far beyond that which is possible to man, filled the disciples with fear. "They were sore amazed in themselves beyond measure, and wondered." But the One whose power is greater than all the storms that men or the devil can raise, is the One Who is for us. He had been praying for them on the mountain, He had seen them toiling, and now He comes to them. Nevertheless, He tries their faith, even as believers are often tested in our day, for we read, He "would have passed them by". His power, His intercession, His loving care, are all at their disposal, but have they the faith to avail themselves of His fulness? In their trouble they cry out, "and immediately He talked with them", saying, "It is I; be not afraid." He may come to them in the glory of His power, above all storms, but He assures them that it is Himself — Jesus, their Saviour, Shepherd, Friend. The One that a little while before men had rejected as only a Carpenter, is now seen to be the Creator who can walk upon the sea, and Whom the winds and the waves obey.

Alas! like ourselves too often, the disciples had not "considered" the greatness of His power and grace displayed on a former occasion. Occupied with themselves and their difficulties their hearts were hardened and little able to avail themselves of their resources in Christ.

VERSES 53-56

The chapter closes with a foretaste of the blessing of a future day when Christ will come again, and through a godly remnant of the Jews bring blessing to the earth. Then indeed the toil of the godly will be over, opposition will end, the storms will cease, and Christ will be received where once He was rejected.

8.
Man Exposed and God Revealed

CHAPTER 7

We have seen in chapter 6, the exposure and condemnation of the social and political world. In this chapter we have the condemnation of the formal religion of the flesh (1-13); the exposure of the heart of man (14-23); and the revelation of the heart of God (24-37).

VERSES 1-5

The chapter opens with the religious leaders of the nation coming to Jesus, not with any sense of their need or of His grace, but, alas! to oppose Christ by finding fault with His disciples because they ate bread with unwashen hands. The religion of these men consisted in honouring the tradition of their ancestors, by the performance of certain outward forms and ceremonies which any one can do, and which make a reputation before men, but leave the heart far from God.

VERSES 6-13

In His reply to these men, the Lord exposes the emptiness of their religion that consists in mere outward forms. First, it leaves men mere *hypocrites*, as proved by Scripture, for Isaiah said of such, "This people honoureth me with their lips, but their heart is far from me." Hypocrisy is pretending to be what we are not. By their religious acts they professed great piety before men, and by their words they professed to reverence God; actually their hearts were far from God (Isaiah 29:13; Ezekiel 33:31).

Secondly, the Lord shows that such religion is "in vain". It may gain for its devotees a reputation for piety before men, but it is worthless in the sight of God.

Thirdly, it sets aside the plain *word of God* in favour of the traditions of men. The Lord gives an example of this great evil. The word of God gives plain directions for the children to honour the parents; but they had a tradition by which they could profess to set aside their property for the use of God by saying "It is Corban", meaning a gift devoted to God, and therefore could not be used to help a needy parent. Thus, by their tradition, they set aside the word of God, evaded their responsibility to their needy relatives, and ministered to their own covetousness.

It adds solemnity to this passage, if we remember that these Pharisees and Scribes from Jerusalem were the religious leaders of the remnant that had been delivered from Babylon. There was indeed, in the Lord's day, a little feeble remnant within this remnant, who feared the Lord, thought upon His Name, and looked for redemption in Israel, but alas! the mass had sunk into the terrible condition set forth by these leaders. They were no longer idolaters. Outwardly they were very pious before men, and with their lips they made a fair profession before God, but we learn that all this is possible and yet the heart be far from God, and the word of God be set aside by the traditions of men.

Verses 14-16

Having exposed the hypocrisy of the outward religion of the flesh, the Lord, in the hearing of "all the people", shows that the source of defilement is not from without, but from within. The washing of hands and cups and pots, simply deals with defilement from without, but the source of moral defilement springs from the inward evil of the heart. This cuts at the root of all worldly religion of the flesh which simply deals with externals and leaves the heart untouched. God works from within and deals with the conscience and heart. The real source of defilement is not a man's environment but himself. It is true that man being such as he is — a fallen creature — if he goes into scenes of evil and temptation, his surroundings will stir up his lusts within. But even so the source of the evil is from within. An Angel can pass through Sodom and not be defiled, but not so Lot. There was no evil heart in the Angel to answer to sin; there was in Lot.

Verses 17-23

Alone with His disciples the Lord enlarges upon this theme, and interprets His illustration. Moral evil has its root in the heart whatever form the evil may take, whether it be *evil thinking*, *evil acts*, such as adulteries, murder, thefts or deceit, *evil looking*, or *evil speaking* in blasphemy, pride and foolishness. "All these evils come from within, and defile the man."

Verses 24-30

The evil of the heart of man being exposed, we have in the story of the Syrophenician woman a blessed unfolding of the heart of God — a heart that, full of love, maintains the truth while dispensing grace to needy sinners. The Lord as He passed through this world that had rejected Him would fain be hid, thus revealing the lowly mind of

Christ that led Him to make Himself of no reputation. But such was His perfection — so great the contrast to all around — that He could not be hid. As one has said, "Goodness joined with power are too rare in the world to remain unnoticed" (J.N.Darby).

The woman was a Greek, that is a Gentile, but her deep need brought her to the Lord. She had faith in the power of Jesus, and in His grace to use the power on behalf of a Gentile dog. The Lord draws out her faith by saying, "Let the children first be filled: for it is not meet to take the children's bread and cast it unto the dogs." This was a great test for faith. She might have argued, "Then I am only a dog and have no claim upon the Lord; the blessing only belongs to the children." Her faith triumphs over this difficulty by admitting the truth as to herself and falling back upon the grace that is in His heart. She can say, as it were, "Yes, as far as I am concerned, it is true I cannot claim the place of a child. I am but a dog, but my whole trust is in what You are and not what I am. I see there is such grace in your heart that you would not deny a crumb to a dog." This is ever the way of faith to own the wretchedness, the vileness, and unworthiness of our hearts, and rest in the perfect grace of His heart. Faith lays hold of Christ and rests upon Who He is and what He has done.

This was a faith that the Lord would not, and could not, deny. He could not say, "I am not so good as you suppose", or "My grace is not so great as you imagine." Blessed be His Name, His grace exceeds all our faith, and He delights to respond to the smallest faith. Thus faith in Christ secures the blessing, and He can say to the woman, "For this saying go thy way; the devil is gone out of thy daughter."

VERSES 31-37

In the closing scene the Lord is found again in Galilee, amongst the people of Israel. They bring to Him one that is deaf and with an impediment in his speech. The man fitly represents the condition to which sin had reduced the nation. Christ is in their midst with grace and power to meet their need, but sin has so blinded them that the nation, as a whole, cannot avail themselves of the healing virtue that is in Christ.

Nevertheless their sin cannot change His heart of love. Hence He will not turn away a case of need. If He will not send away a Gentile woman, neither will He refuse an appeal on behalf of a needy Jew. But in dispensing grace, He will, in both cases, maintain truth. So we read, "He took him aside from the multitude." He is not indifferent to their rejection of Himself. If He works in their midst it is because of their need, and not because they are Jews. Sin has put Jew and Gentile on one common level, and grace can bless either on the ground of their need.

In showing grace the Lord looked up to heaven and sighed. He ever acted in dependence upon the Father and in accord with the mind of heaven. His heart was sustained by heaven if it was broken by the sorrows of earth. We, too, as the sorrows of earth press upon our spirits may well sigh; but, too often, we sigh without *looking up to heaven*, and so become cast down and depressed. Looking around we sigh; but looking up we are sustained. Having healed the man He charges them that they should tell no man. He was here as the perfect Servant, so would not use His mighty power and grace to exalt Himself. His mind was to make Himself of no reputation. But He could not be hid. The people were beyond measure astonished and said, "He hath done all things well: He maketh both the deaf to hear, and the dumb to speak."

9.
Christic in the Outside Place

CHAPTER 8

In the previous chapters, 6 and 7, we have seen that the presence of the Lord Jesus, in the midst of men, had made manifest the corruption and unbelief of the social, political, and religious world. Every overture of grace being rejected the Lord retires from the haunts of men and is found apart in "the desert place", alone on "a mountain", and "walking upon the sea" (Mark 6:31, 46, 48).

In chapter 8, the Lord identifies His own with Himself in this outside place, and exhorts them to follow Him (1, 10, 27, 34). Further we learn the fulness of the resources in Christ for those who follow Him in the path of separation. Their needs are met (1-9); opposers are silenced (10-13); spiritual vision is given to see all things clearly (14-26). Moreover while we are warned that to follow Christ through a world from which He is rejected, will entail suffering, reproach, and present loss, we are also encouraged by the prospect of the glory of the Kingdom to which the path of suffering leads. If we suffer with Him. we shall also reign with Him.

Verses 1-9

The former miracle in which the Lord fed the five thousand, had a distinctly dispensational bearing, as it became a solemn witness that the One the nation rejected was their true Messiah. It is immediately followed by the Lord taking a place on the mountain as intercessor, while His disciples are left to face the opposition of the world — a picture, surely of Christ's present service on high on behalf of His people.

This second miracle of feeding the multitude has a more distinctly moral significance as setting forth, not only the resources that are in the Lord to meet the needs of His people, but also the compassion of His heart that feels for those whose needs He meets. The disciples do not come to the Lord, as in the former miracle, calling His attention to the people's needs. Here everything proceeds from the Lord. He sees the need; He calls the disciples to Himself; He brings before them His compassion; He sets the people in rest, making them to sit down; He takes what is to hand, and giving thanks for it, distributes it to the people through the disciples, and thus satisfies their need.

Let us remember that He is the same today. He knows our needs, and has the heart to love and the hand to nourish and cherish His people (Ephesians 5:23, 25, 29). Too often, like the disciples, we feel the need and the utter inadequacy of the little we have to meet it. If, however, like the Lord, we bring our little into touch with heaven and give thanks for it, should we not find that God can make it go a long way, and not only meet our need, but even have something in hand?

Verses 10-13

On a previous occasion when the disciples entered a ship, the Lord went up into a mountain to intercede for them

(6:45-47). On this second occasion the Lord went "with His disciples", setting forth the further truth that, He is not only *for* us on high, but, *with* us to support us in the storms of life, and in meeting the opposition of the enemy. This opposition is ever directed against Christ: so we read that having come to land the Pharisees "began to dispute *against Him*" (N.Tr.). Already signs in abundance had been given; therefore to ask for a further sign only betrayed the enmity and unbelief of the flesh. The wickedness of man, however, became an occasion for revealing the perfection of the heart of Christ. Their malicious opposition aroused no angry resentment in the Lord, as too often some little opposition may do with ourselves. With Him it was met with feelings of sorrow and pity, for we read, "He sighed deeply in His spirit." He asks the searching question, "Why doth this generation seek after a sign?" Signs are of no avail, and proofs useless, to those who, moved by malice refuse to believe. Such seal their own doom, for we read that the Lord "left them and … departed to the other side." Solemn, indeed when men leave the Lord; but how far more terrible the condition of those from whom the Lord departs.

Verses 14-21

Upon entering the ship the second time we learn that the disciples had forgotten to take bread, and what was more serious had forgotten the grace and power of the Lord that had met the needs of hungry multitudes. Occupied with their material needs they fail to understand the warning of the Lord against the leaven of the Pharisees and the leaven of Herod. Though associated with Christ in a path apart from the corrupt world, they were, as with believers today, in danger of being leavened with the time-serving spirit of the political world which marked the Herodians, or the form of godliness without the power that marked the Pharisees.

As so often with ourselves, the disciples reason about the Lord's words and miss their spiritual import by materialising them and seeking to reduce them to the level of the human understanding. The Lord rebukes them for their lack of spiritual perception, and short memory of His grace and power. He asks some searching question which we may well address to ourselves. "Why reason ye?" Why "perceive ye not yet, neither understand?" "Have ye your heart yet hardened?" "Do ye not remember?"

Instead of facing facts, and listening to the truth, we, at times "reason"; and our natural reasoning obscures our spiritual understanding. Behind the darkness of nature there is, too often, the hardness of heart which comes from so quickly forgetting the grace and love of His heart — we do "not remember". These searching questions have a voice for all believers, for they were uttered, not to opposers, but, to true disciples.

Verses 22-26

The case of the blind man clearly sets forth the difference between the nation and the disciples. The nation, as such, were in total blindness. The disciples, though true believers in the Lord, at that time lacked spiritual intelligence. They saw but dimly His Divine glory. They recognised and owned Him as the true Messiah, but their Jewish prejudices, and habits of thought hindered them from seeing fully His further glories as the Son of Man and Son of God. For this they needed to be wholly separated from the nation; and hence the significance of the Lord's act in leading the man out of the town, as before He had taken the deaf and dumb man aside from the multitude.

At the first touch the man's sight was received, but he had not at once the skill to use the sight. He said, "I see men as trees walking." The disciples were in like condition spiritually. They were hindered from discerning the glory of the Lord by having an exalted sense of the greatness and importance of man. We need, not only the grace that gives sight, but the further grace to use the sight that we may see "every man clearly" — to see men as they really are, and to see ourselves in all our weakness, and above all to see Jesus in all His perfection.

The Lord sends the man to his house. He was not to return to the town, nor tell it to any in the town. The time for testimony to the nation at large was over.

VERSES 27-33

The discourse of the Lord with His disciples that follows, shows, not only the unbelief of the natural man, but how little the true disciples discerned His true mission and glory. The great test question then, as now, is "Who do men say that I am?" All glory for God and blessing for man turns upon the Person of Christ. It becomes manifest that mere human intelligence will never arrive at the truth. The men of that day included many scholars with great intellectual abilities, nevertheless all their thoughts about Christ ended in speculation and uncertainty. Some said He was John the Baptist, others that He was Elias, others again that He was one of the prophets. None arrived at the truth. In contrast we see in Peter the result of simple faith in one that was an ignorant and unlearned man when measured against the intellectual leaders of this world. Faith does not speculate or reason, but with the utmost certainty arrives at the truth, for faith is the gift of God. Thus Peter can say, "Thou art the Christ."

The Lord charged them that they should tell no man of Him. He had been rejected by the nation, so His position as the Messiah is for the time set aside and the Lord takes the wider title of Son of Man which leads to greater glories than earthly dominion in connection with Israel, for as Son of Man He will have universal dominion over all created things. But before He can take His place as Son of Man with all things put in subjection under Him, and exercise His grace towards all men, He must go into death, accomplish redemption and break the power of Satan, death and the grave. With the cross in view He began to teach His disciples that the Son of Man must suffer many things, be rejected and killed, and after three days rise again. Of this great truth the time had come to speak openly to the disciples, and no longer in parables.

At once it becomes manifest that though the disciples had true faith in Christ, yet, like the man with the partially recovered sight they but dimly discerned the glory of the Lord as the Son of Man. Peter could not endure the thought that His Master and Lord should be despised and rejected of men, and so rebuked the Lord. Knowing the effect that Peter's words would have upon the disciples, the Lord, looking upon them, "Rebuked Peter, saying, Get thee behind me Satan: for thy mind is not on the things that be of God, but the things that be of men" (N.Tr.). How solemn that, as true believers, it is possible to make statements with the utmost sincerity which come from Satan. Peter may have thought he was only expressing a loving sentiment for His Master; actually he was doing the work of Satan by seeking to turn the Lord from the path of obedience to the Father's will, and casting a stumbling block in the way of the disciples. He was viewing all from a merely human standpoint. At the moment he saw men as trees walking.

VERSES **34-38**

The Lord having called the people unto Him, with His disciples, leads their thoughts from "the things that be of men" by instructing them in the mind of God. If they would follow Him into the new world of blessing and glory that He was opening up as the Son of Man, they must be prepared for His position of suffering and rejection in this world. Here it is no question of expiatory suffering when forsaken by God, but of meeting the contradiction of sinners and suffering from the hands of men, in which, in some little measure, believers can share even to a martyr's death. To follow Christ in a world from which He has been rejected will mean that self must be denied, the present life let go, and the world refused. But whatever the path involves in this world, it leads to the day of glory when the Son of Man will come in the glory of His Father with the holy angels.

Contemplating the Lord Jesus as presented in this chapter, we see Him in the outside place with His own, having a perfect knowledge of our needs, with a heart that feels for us in our needs, and a hand that provides for our needs. Moreover to follow Him will mean that we, not only walk *where* He walked — in the outside place, but that we walk *as* He walked. In our little measure we shall have hearts moved with compassion for the needs of others; we shall give thanks for God's mercies, and we shall meet the opposition of those who dispute against us, in no spirit of resentment, but with sorrow of heart. We, too, shall deny ourselves, accept the path of reproach, refusing the life here and the present evil world, while looking on to the glory of the world to come, even as He, for the joy that was set before Him endured the cross, despising the shame, and is set down at the right hand of God (Hebrews 12:2, 3).

10.
The Power of the World to Come

CHAPTER 9

As the disciples beheld the grace, and love, and power of the Lord Jesus in relieving men of their distresses, they saw, indeed, something of the blessedness of the Kingdom of God, but in circumstances of weakness, for the King was in their midst as a poor Man, despised and rejected of men, with not where to lay His head. In order to sustain their faith, and ours, in following a rejected Christ in His lowly path of suffering and reproach, the Lord passes before us a vision of the coming glory to show that the path of outward weakness will end in "the Kingdom of God come with *power*".

VERSES 2-3

To see this glorious vision, the Lord leads Peter, and James, and John into an "high mountain apart by themselves". And, if, as believers, we are "To look beyond the long dark night, And hail the coming day", we, too, shall need, in spirit, to be lifted above the turmoil of this poor world, to find ourselves alone with Jesus. In such moments, as with the disciples, our souls will, above all else, be engaged with the glory of His Person. Thus, in this vision, the disciples are first arrested by the glory of the Lord; "He was transfigured before them." In after years, Peter, writing of this great scene, can say, "We made known unto you the power and coming of our Lord Jesus Christ." They say, not only His coming, but "the power" of His coming. They saw a sample of the mighty power that at His coming will change us into His likeness in the twinkling of an eye. In a moment He was "transfigured", and His garments of humiliation were changed into shining raiment "exceeding white as snow".

Verse 4

Further we learn that in His reign of glory and power there will be associated with Him, not only the saints of the present period, represented by the three apostles, but also all believers who lived before the Lord came to earth, represented, in the vision, by Moses and Elias, the two outstanding witnesses to God in the times of the law and the prophets.

Verses 5-8

These witnesses will be associated with Christ in His earthly glory; but, however great in their day, they must give place to Christ. His personal glory is maintained as the One who is supreme. From the nation He had received dishonour and shame. From ignorant but true disciples He receives little more than the honour and glory they would give to Moses and Elias, for Peter would put the Lord on the same level with these great servants. Later, when the Holy Spirit had come, Peter sees the true significance of this great scene, for, he says, the Lord Jesus "received from God the Father honour and glory, when there came such a voice to Him from the excellent glory, This is my beloved Son in whom I am well pleased." The honour that He received from the Father, and heaven —

the excellent glory — is in contrast to what He received from man, the world, and even true disciples. In our day, are believers not in danger, at times, of falling into the snare of forgetting that, however outstanding the devotedness and spirituality of individual servants may be, the Lord is supreme? They may change and pass away; but of the Lord alone it can be said, "Thou remainest", and "Thou art the Same". Thus with the disciples, having heard the voice from heaven, saying, "This is my beloved Son: hear Him", "they saw no man any more, save Jesus only". Moreover, they saw that He was *with themselves*. They had just seen two men "with Jesus" in glory: now they see Jesus "with themselves", in the path that leads to glory. Good, for us, to realise the glory of the Person of Jesus — the One that we shall be *with* in the glory, and that He is *with us* on the way to glory.

VERSES 9-10

To make this possible the blessed Lord must die and rise again from among the dead. So, in a later day an apostle can write, "He died for us, that whether we wake or sleep, we should *live together with Him*" (1 Thessalonians 5:10). At that time this great truth raised a difficulty in the minds of the disciples. They believed in a general resurrection at the last day (John 11:24); but that any one should rise from among the dead leaving others in their graves for a later resurrection was something entirely foreign to their thoughts. This, however, is the fundamental truth of Christianity. The resurrection of Christ *from among* the dead is the everlasting proof of God's acceptance of His work, and that believers are accepted in Him, and will share in the first resurrection of the just. So we read, "Every man in his own order: Christ the firstfruits; afterward they that are Christ's at His coming" (1 Corinthians 15:23).

Alas! as with ourselves, too often, when faced with difficulties, they kept the difficulty "*with themselves*, questioning *one with another*", instead of spreading their difficulty before the Lord.

VERSES 11-13

The disciples, however, have another difficulty about which they do speak to the Lord. The scribes said that Elias must first come, but apparently Elias had not preceded the Lord. The difficulty arose from the fact that while they accepted the Scriptures that spoke of Christ coming in glory, they overlooked those that spoke of His coming to suffer as the Son of Man. The prophecy of Malachi stated that Elias would precede Christ's coming in glory. This prophecy will surely be fulfilled. Nevertheless, morally he had already come in the forerunner, John the Baptist, who came in the spirit of Elias calling the people to repentance (see Matthew 11:14).

VERSES 14-19

In the former chapter the Pharisees "dispute against" Christ (8:11 N.Tr.). Coming down from the Mount, the Lord finds the scribes "disputing against" His disciples (N.Tr.). Later, the Lord reminds us that, "The servant is not greater than his Lord", and He adds, "If they have persecuted Me, they will also persecute you" (John 15:20). Little wonder, if men dare to "dispute against" Christ, they are opposed to believers. With the Lord this opposition only drew out His perfection; but with us, too often, it exposes our weakness. So, in this scene, having caught a vision of the glory of the Lord on the top of the Mount, we find the misery of man, the power of Satan, and the weakness of the disciples at the foot of the Mount.

When the Lord sent forth the Twelve, He "gave them power over unclean spirits", and for a time they used this power, for we read, "they cast out many devils" (6:7, 13). Here, however, their faith failed. They could not cast out the dumb spirit. There was power present to work miracles, and overcome all the power of Satan, but man could not profit by it, and the disciples had no faith to use it.

In the presence of this failure, the Lord has to say, "O faithless generation, how long shall I be with you? how long shall I suffer you?" — words that indicate the solemn import of the failure of the disciples. It meant that the testimony of God through the disciples had fallen to the ground, and, as a result, the dispensation would come to an end. "How long shall I be with you?" implies that a limit was set to the Lord's sojourn on earth. A needy generation, oppressed by the power of the devil would not drive the Lord away: on the contrary, it was the deep need of man, under the power of Satan, that brought the Lord Jesus into the world. "Christ Jesus came into the world to save sinners." It is the "faithless generation", not the needy generation, that brings His mission of grace and power on the earth to an end. When there is no longer power to use the resources in Christ, His service on earth is finished.

Has this not a voice for Christians, for again, is it not the failure of God's people, rather than the increasing wickedness of the world, that is bringing this day of grace to its close? That which professes to be a public witness for Christ on the earth in its last phase becomes so nauseous to Christ that He has to say, "I will spue thee out of my mouth."

Nevertheless, the goodness of the Lord is not withered up by the opposition of man, or the failure of His own, for the Lord can add the comforting words, concerning the demon possessed man, "*Bring him unto Me.*" As one has said, "Faith however small it be, is never left without an answer from the Lord. What a consolation! Whatever be the unbelief, not only of the world, but of Christians — if only one solitary person were left in the world who had faith in the goodness and power of the Lord Jesus he could not come to Him with a real need, and simple belief, without finding His heart ready and His power sufficient." As, in the presence of the failure of His own disciples, He could say on earth, "Bring him unto Me", so in the last solemn moments when the Lord is about to spue the professing church out of His mouth, He can say, "Behold, I stand at the door, and knock: if any man hear My voice, and open the door, I will come into him, and will sup with him, and he with Me." However dark the day, however great our failure, Christ is the Same, and Christ remains. He still stands at the door, and is ready to bless "any man" that hears His voice and opens the door to Him. May it be our happy lot to respond to His voice, and say,

> *O Lord and Saviour, we recline*
> *On that eternal love of Thine,*
> *Thou art our rest, and Thou alone*
> *Remainest when all else is gone.*

Verses 20-27

In response to the Lord's words, they brought the case of need "unto Him". But, as too often with ourselves, they come with feeble faith in the power of the Lord, for the poor father says, "If Thou canst do anything, have compassion on us, and help us." The Lord in His reply says, "The 'if thou couldest' is 'if thou couldest believe': all things are possible to him that believes" (N.Tr.). One has truly remarked on these words, "Power connects itself with faith; the difficulty is not in Christ's power, but in man's believing; all things were possible if he could believe. This is an important principle; Christ's power never fails to accomplish all that is good for man; faith alas! may be wanting in us to profit by it" (J.N.Darby).

VERSES **28-29**

Alone with His disciples, in the house, we learn from the Lord the deeply important truth that the faith which uses the Lord in all our difficulties can alone be sustained by intimate communion with God, set forth by prayer, and abstinence from the things of the world, set forth by fasting. As with the disciples, so with ourselves, behind our lack of faith to use the power of the Lord there is a lack of communion in prayer with the Lord.

VERSES **30-32**

The glory of the Kingdom had been revealed; the power and grace of the Lord to bring in the blessings of the Kingdom had been manifested, only to bring out the unbelief of the world, and the failure of His own to use the power in their midst. His departure was at hand, and the time for all public appeal to the nation, as a whole, had gone by. He will, indeed, dispense grace to individual need, but the reigning time had not yet come, so, as He went through the land, "He would not that any man should know it." The sin of man was about to rise to its height in killing the Son of Man. But this would become the occasion of manifesting the mighty power of Christ over sin, and Satan, and death, by rising from the dead. The Lord's words again manifest the weakness of the disciples. They not only lacked spiritual intelligence to understand the truth of the resurrection, but they "were afraid to ask Him". In the matter of the man with the evil spirit their faith was too weak to use the *power* of Christ; now their confidence is too small to use the *wisdom* in Christ. Alas! how often, like the disciples, when difficulties arise, we seek solution by discussing them "one with another" (verse 10), instead of turning to Christ, our Head, with Whom is all wisdom.

VERSES 33-34

Alone in the house with His own, the Lord, by a simple question, reaches the conscience of His disciples, and exposes the root of much of their weakness. By the way they had disputed among themselves, and the subject of the dispute was "who should be the greatest". Alas! since that day, how often the desire to be the greatest has been the real root of many a dispute among the people of God. Whatever the immediate question under discussion, underneath there has often been a great deal of self in the dispute; for self not only wants to be great, it wants to be "the greatest". If a believer wants to be the greatest, sooner or later it will lead to a dispute in which any little slip in a brother will be seized upon in the endeavour to belittle him in order to exalt self. The very thought of being great shows how little the disciples comprehended the truth of the Kingdom. They failed to see that the Kingdom is for the display of all that God is in love, righteousness, grace and power. So too, in our day, we may fall into the snare of using the assembly as a sphere in which to exalt ourselves. The Corinthians were doing so by means of gifts, and carnal methods: the Galatians were doing so by legality; and the Colossians were in danger of doing so by fleshly religion.

If, however, believers can dispute *among themselves*, they have to hold their peace *in the presence of the Lord*. We may be sure that when believers start disputing among themselves, they are no longer consciously in His presence.

74

VERSE 35

With infinite patience, the Lord instructs His disciples. In the presence of their heartlessness that sought their own greatness at the very moment when He had reminded them that He was about to be killed, He does not rise up with indignation and leave them, but "He sat down, and called the twelve" around Him, and gently instructs them in the path of true greatness. If any one desires to be first in the Kingdom, let them be last in the path that leads to glory — let them become the "servant of all". We might be prepared at times to serve some great person, or some devoted saint, and exalt ourselves by so doing; but are we prepared to be the "servant *of all?*" It has been truly said, that "Love is the most powerful of all things, and loves to minister, not to be ministered to", and again, "He who is smallest in his own eyes is the greatest" (J.N.Darby).

VERSES 36-37

Having instructed the disciples in the path of true greatness, the Lord illustrates His instruction by placing a little child in their midst and showing how He, Himself, could stoop to taking a little child into His arms of love. The disciple who can receive one of such little children, in His Name, will be following the Lord in the path of true greatness. He will be stooping to the lowest in the Name of the Highest. So doing he will find himself in company with Christ, and to receive Christ is to receive the One that sent Him. Thus refusing self, and self-exaltation, we shall find ourselves in company with Divine Persons.

VERSES 38-41

We have seen the danger of exalting self; in the incident that follows we see another snare, the danger of exalting a company. John says, "Teacher, we saw one casting out demons in thy Name, and he followeth not us: and we forbade him, *because he followeth not us.*" They themselves, though following with Christ, had just failed, through lack of prayer and fasting, to cast out a demon. Now they forbid one to do, what they had failed to do because he followed not with them. The Lord in his answer, shows that what is of value, above all else, in His sight, is the disciple's relation to Himself. It may be true that the man had not the faith to identify himself with the disciples who were following the Lord in the outside path; but, if he could do a miracle in Christ's Name it was evident he set value on that Name and would not speak lightly of it.

So absolutely had the world rejected Christ that there would be none in that circle but opposers of Christ. If there are any not against Christ they must belong to those who are on His part, even if they lacked the faith to publicly identify themselves with Him. John had said they are not "with us", but, even so, the Lord can say they are "*not against us*". The disciples were making too much of this wretched "us" — the weak little company gathered round Christ — and too little of Christ — the glorious Person to Whom they were gathered. The Lord reminds them that His Name is everything. The smallest act, even to giving a cup of cold water to one that belongs to Christ, if done in His Name will not lose its reward.

VERSES 42-48

Warnings follow. Let us beware that in condemning others that we are not putting a stumbling block in the path of one of Christ's little ones. Further, let us see to it that we deal faithfully with every evil tendency in ourselves, by refusing all that would lead into sin. This may entail the stern refusal of that which is most precious to the flesh — the hand, the foot, and the eye, and every form of evil into which these members can lead us. Let us not forget that these evils are taking men on to the never ending judgment.

VERSES **49-50**

All will be put to the proof. The fire will try both saints and sinners, "Every one shall be salted with fire, and every sacrifice shall be salted with salt." The sinner that rejects Christ will pass into the fire that is not quenched: but the true saint will be tested by fire that will take the form of trials or even persecution. The apostle Peter tells us that our faith may be tried with fire, and warns us not to think it strange if we are passed through a "fiery trial" but rather to rejoice, inasmuch as if we partake of "Christ's sufferings" we shall also share in "His glory" (1 Peter 1:7; 4:12, 13). The believer's life here is also viewed as a sacrifice, for we are to present our "bodies a living sacrifice, holy, acceptable unto God" (Romans 12:1). But the sacrifice is to be kept pure, "salted with salt". The Christian, if practically holy, becomes a witness in the midst of the world. Apart from holiness, his life is like salt that has lost its savour. We are to have salt in ourselves and walk in peace with others.

In the course of the chapter we see, on the one hand, the perfections of Christ, and on the other, the exposure of what the flesh is even in true disciples — those who loved and followed the Lord. In the presence of the glory the disciples were "sore afraid" (6): in the presence of the power of Satan they lacked the faith to use the power that was at their disposal in Christ (18, 19): behind this lack of faith there was the neglect of prayer and fasting (29): being little in communion with God in prayer, when difficulties arose in their minds they discussed them one with another, but were afraid to ask Him (10, 32): out of touch with Christ, they disputed among themselves, each seeking to be the greatest, and condemned what another was doing in the name of Christ because he was not in their company (38).

If, however, we see our own weakness in the disciples, we see the fulness of our resources in Christ. We see on top of the Mount the glory and power of the Kingdom, and that we shall be *with Him* in the glory. At the bottom of the Mount we see amidst all our weakness and difficulties He is *with us* our unfailing resource, the One to Whom we are invited to bring every trial and all our hard questions (19, 33): the One who is our teacher (31), to whose Name we gather (39), and who will reward the smallest act done in His Name (41).

11.
Suffering and Glory

CHAPTER 10:1-45

In this portion of the gospel three important principles are brought before us:- First, we learn that the Lord owns natural relationships as originally established by God, and creature goodness. Marriage is respected (2-12); children are recognised (13-16); and natural uprightness and amiability are acknowledged (17-22). Secondly, we see that the natural relationships that have been established and owned by God, have become corrupted by man. The marriage relationship has been marred by the hardness of man's heart (5); children are despised as of small account (13), and natural integrity and earthly possessions are used to separate the soul from God, and hinder men from entering into the Kingdom of God (22, 23). Thirdly, such being the failure of the natural man, those that follow Christ into the kingdom, must, in this present world, be prepared for suffering. However great the earthly riches, the one that follows Christ must take up the cross (21); face persecution (30), and be prepared to take a lowly place in this world, in view of the world to come (44). Of

79

such a path, Christ, as the lowly Servant, is the perfect example (33, 34, 45).

Verses 1-12

The relationship of marriage is introduced by the Pharisees coming to the Lord with the question, "Is it lawful for a man to put away his wife?" Evidently they had no real desire to learn the truth, for we read, they were "tempting Him". Apparently they hoped that by the Lord's answer they would be able either to accuse Him of ignoring what Moses said, or else sanctioning the loose customs that prevailed amongst the people. As usual, when men in their folly seek to tempt the Lord they themselves are thoroughly exposed.

The Lord meets the question, "Is it lawful?" by appealing to the law. "What did Moses command you?" In their reply they sought to turn aside the Lord's question by speaking, not of what Moses commanded, but of what Moses *allowed* (N.Tr.). So doing they unwittingly exposed the hardness of their hearts. They neglected the positive commands of Moses, and speak only of special precepts instituted to meet their own hardness. The commands met God's heart for man; the precepts as to divorce were to meet their hearts.

Having exposed the hardness of man's heart the Lord presents the truth of the marriage relationship according to the creation order established by God from the beginning. Thus the Lord puts His sanction upon the marriage tie, and enables the Christian to take up the relationship according to the order of creation and not according to the precepts of men.

In the house the Lord further instructs His disciples as to the solemnity of annulling the marriage tie in order to indulge the desires of the flesh towards another woman. In God's sight this is to fall into the most degrading sin.

VERSES 13-16

In the next incident we see that even the disciples were strangers to the mind of the Lord as to little children. Apparently they thought the Lord was too great to notice these little ones, and they too insignificant to attract His attention. In rebuking those who brought their young children to be blessed by the Lord they entirely misrepresented their Master, failed to see what is beautiful in a child, and denied the principles of the Kingdom that they professed to preach.

The action of the disciples arouses the righteous indignation of the Lord. He meets their poor thoughts by saying, "Suffer the little children to come unto Me, and forbid them not: for of such is the kingdom of God." There is a welcome in His heart for the weak and simple. Even though the root of sin be in them, yet their simplicity and confidence are the outstanding marks of those who enter the Kingdom of God. And even as He took these little ones into His arms and blessed them, so will the everlasting arms be under all those who in simplicity and confidence put their trust in Him, and His hands be lifted up to bless them (Deuteronomy 33:2, 7; Luke 24:50).

VERSES 17-22

In the incident that follows we learn that creature excellence, and earthly possessions, however right in their place, not only can give no entrance into the Kingdom of God, but may be a real barrier to blessing. Nature at its best has no sense of its need of Christ, and no true apprehension of the glory of Christ.

There was much that was excellent in this rich man. He was full of youthful ardour for he came "running". He was ready to admit the superiority of Christ for he reverently "kneeled" to Him. He was desirous to do right, for he asks, "What shall I do?" Outwardly his character was excellent. He had not been depraved by the indulgence of sin. He had kept the outward law. There was much that was lovely in his character — the fruit of creation — that called forth the Lord's esteem and love. As one has said, "He was amiable and well disposed and ready to learn that which is good; he had witnessed the excellence of the life and works of Jesus and his heart was touched at what he had seen" (J.N.Darby).

Yet all this natural excellence left him without any true appreciation of the Person and glory of Christ, or any true sense of the state and need of his own heart. He could discern the pre-eminent excellence of Christ as a Man, but he could not discern the glory of His Person as the Son of God. Nature, however excellent, cannot discern God is Christ. So the Lord can say to Peter, on another occasion, "Blessed art thou … for *flesh and blood* hath not revealed it unto thee, but my Father which is in heaven." The Lord, taking the young man up on his own ground, will not admit that man is good, "There is none good but one, that is, God." Christ, indeed, was good, but He was God. "He was always God, and God became man without ceasing to be, or being able to cease being, God" (J.N.Darby).

Moreover, having no sense of his need, the young man does not ask "What must I do to be saved?" but "What shall I do that I may inherit eternal life?" His fine natural disposition blinded him to the fact that, in spite of all his good qualities he was a lost sinner in need of salvation. The Lord draws aside the veil and exposes the true state of his heart, by telling him to "Go, sell that thou hast, and come and follow Me." This brings to light the solemn fact that in spite of his amiable and excellent character, he had a heart that prefers money to Christ; thus we read, "He was sad and went away grieved." How entirely this proves there is no good in man for God. An excellent character is no indication of the moral state of the heart. Truly one has written, "The thing that governs the heart, its motive, is the true measure of man's moral state, and not the qualities which he possesses by birth, however pleasing these may be. Good qualities are to be found even in animals; they are to be esteemed, but they do not at all reveal the moral state of the heart" (J.N.Darby).

Christ, Himself was the perfect example of the course that He proposed for the young Man. "Ye know the grace of our Lord Jesus Christ, that though He was rich, yet for your sakes He became poor, that ye through His poverty might be rich" (2 Corinthians 8:9). Not discerning the glory of the Lord, this young man failed to see His grace. We never see His *grace* until we have seen His glory.

Verses 23-27

Knowing the effect of His words upon the disciples, the Lord, as He looks upon them, presses home the lesson we are to learn from this young man, by saying, "How hardly shall they that have riches enter into the kingdom of God!" These words were an astonishment to the disciples, who, with their Jewish thoughts of earthly blessing looked upon riches and possessions as a mark of God's favour. Moreover the thought in their heart, as with ourselves too often, was possibly, if only we had riches how much good we might be able to do. To meet these difficulties the Lord shows that the great danger of riches lies in the fact that men think they can secure salvation and the blessings of the Kingdom by means of riches, and thus put their *trust* in riches. Let us note that the Lord does not speak of a literally rich man, but of *one that trusts in riches*. This is a danger to which the poorest in actual possessions is exposed equally with the one who possesses most. The Lord uses a figure to show how difficult it is for a rich man to enter the Kingdom of God. With astonishment the disciples ask, "Who then can be saved?" In reply the Lord tells us, "With men it is impossible, but not with God." Their question would indicate that the thought lingered in their minds that in some measure at least their salvation depended upon themselves. They had to learn, as we all have to learn, that our salvation is wholly the work of God, and not of man at all. Neither law nor nature, riches or poverty have any part in the saving of the soul. Salvation rests wholly in the power of God's grace, and what is impossible for man is possible with God. Thus we read, "*By grace* are ye saved *through faith*; and that not of yourselves: it is the gift of God: not of works, lest any man should boast" (Ephesians 2:4-9).

VERSES 28-31

Peter suggests that the twelve had taken the course that the Lord had set before the young man, and asks, as it were, what they should have? The Lord replies that they would gain a hundredfold now in this time, with persecutions, and in the coming age eternal life. If we leave the circle of our unconverted and natural relations, we shall find we are in the far larger circle of the family of God. This may result in a measure of persecution from the world circle that we have left, but it is the pathway into life. The Lord's words, however, indicate that it is not the mere fact of leaving all that will be rewarded, but doing so from a right motive. It must not be done to exalt self, or even gain a reward but as the Lord says, "For my sake and the gospel's."

The Lord adds a searching word, "But many that are first shall be last; and the last first." This would surely be a warning word against the self-complacency to which we are all so prone, and which apparently marked the words of Peter when he said, "Lo, we have left all." What, indeed, had he left, but a few old nets that wanted mending! Let us beware of boasting in what we have given up for Christ. It has been well said, "It is not the beginning of the race that decides the contest; the end of it is necessarily the great point. In that race there are many changes, and withal not a few slips, falls and reverses." The real question is not what we have left in the past, but what are we doing today?

VERSES 32-34

The twelve had left all to follow Christ; but so little had they counted the cost, that at once they find themselves in a path that fills them with fear. "They were amazed" as they see the Lord deliberately taking a path that will involve trial and persecution, and they were afraid for themselves. The Lord does not hide from them the sufferings He was about to face. He tells them that as the Son of Man he was about to be delivered up to the leaders of the Nation and of the Gentiles, who would heap every insult upon Him, and kill Him, but after three days He would rise again.

VERSES 35-45

At that time the Lord could not find one amongst the twelve who could enter into His mind, feel with Him, or understand the need of His sufferings. Possessed with the thought of a kingdom on earth, James and John come forward with a desire for a high position, close to the Lord's Person, in the kingdom. There was true faith that the kingdom was going to be established, but, as so often with ourselves, there was a good deal of unjudged flesh intruding into the realm of faith. They viewed the kingdom as an opportunity for their own advancement, rather than as the sphere for the display of the glory of Christ. "That which is born of the flesh is flesh", whether it be in obscure saints or leading apostles; and how often since that time has the ugliness of the flesh especially betrayed itself in those that seem to be somewhat.

The Lord turns this fleshly question into an occasion for instruction. He presses that the path to the glory of the kingdom is through suffering. He alone could accomplish redemption by the sufferings of the cross when forsaken by God. But the disciples should have the privilege of drinking the cup of suffering from the hands of men. Moreover if He could assure to them the privilege of suffering for His Name's sake, He could not give them a place at His right hand in the kingdom. He had taken the place of the Servant, and He leaves to the Father to say who shall have a place of special privilege in the day of glory.

Furthermore, the flesh betrays itself in the ten whose indignation with James and John proved that jealousy was at work in their own hearts. One has said, "It is not alone by the fault of one or another that the flesh becomes apparent, but how do we behave ourselves in the presence of the displayed faults of others? The indignation that broke out in the ten shewed the pride of their own hearts, just as much as the two desiring the best place."

Jesus calls them to Himself and corrects the fleshly thoughts of the two disciples and the ten, by setting before them the path of true greatness. If He cannot give them the chief place in glory, He can shew them the path that leads there. The One who takes the lowest place on earth as the bondman of all, will have the highest place in glory. Of such a path the Son of Man was the perfect pattern.

12.
Rejection of the King

CHAPTER 10:46 TO 11:26

In each of the first three Gospels the Lord's entry into Jerusalem, and the miracle by which sight is given to the blind man, introduces the closing events that lead to His death and resurrection. His life upon earth as the Son of Man who came to minister in lowly grace is finished. Now He presents Himself to Jerusalem as the Son of David — the promised Messiah. His rejection as the perfect Servant of Jehovah is followed by His rejection as the Son of David, and both prepare the way for His yet greater service of giving His life as a ransom for many as the Son of Man.

CHAPTER 10 VERSES 46-52

The Lord enters Jericho — the city of the curse — not in judgment to execute the curse, but in lowly grace that was about to bear the curse. Passing out of the city we hear of a blind man sitting by the wayside begging. May we not say that the physical condition of the blind man sets forth the moral condition of the nation? The Messiah was present with grace and power to bless, but the nation, as such, was blind both to the glory of His Person, and to its own deep need. All they could see in Jesus was a despised Nazarene.

In contrast to the crowd, Bartimaeus was conscious of his need, and his own helplessness to meet his need. As ever it is the needy soul that is attracted to Jesus, and that discerns His glory. The people may speak of Jesus as a Nazarene, but faith can discern in that lowly Man the Son of David, the One of whom it is written that He would "open the blind eyes" (Isaiah 42:7). Thus the blind man can "cry out, and say, Jesus, Thou Son of David, have mercy on me."

As ever, when a soul is seeking Jesus there will be hindrances to overcome. Many would have the blind man hold his peace, and not have the Lord disturbed by a beggar. But faith rising above every hindrance, cried out the more a great deal, and grace on the part of the Lord "stood still" and commanded him to be called. Casting away his garment, he rose and came to Jesus. Good, indeed, when conscious of our need, and discerning something of the glory of Jesus, we cast away the garment of any righteousness of our own in which we might trust, and come to Jesus just as we are, in all our need and helplessness. Very blessedly, when the Lord asks, "What wilt thou that I should do unto thee?" the blind man replies, "That I might receive my sight." The Lord takes the place of the *doer*, and the blind man accepts the place of the *receiver*. At once the Lord acknowledges this simple faith. The blind man receives his sight and "followed Jesus in the way", from henceforth to be His disciple. He did not attempt to follow Jesus in order to receive his sight; but having received the blessing he became a follower. We must first receive the blessings of salvation and forgiveness through what Christ has done before we can follow Him as an object for our soul's delight.

CHAPTER 11 VERSES 1-6

Having come nigh to Jerusalem, preparation is made for the Lord's presentation to Israel as the Son of David in fulfilment of the prophecy of Zechariah (Zechariah 9:9). This was a fresh witness to the glory of the Lord and a last testimony to the people. Coming as the King He acts with kingly authority. If any question is raised as to why the disciples were loosening the colt, it would be sufficient to reply "that the Lord hath need of him", and straightway every question would cease. So it came to pass and so will it be in the coming day of glory, when it will be true of Zion that "Thy people shall be willing in the day of thy power" (Psalm 110:3).

VERSES 7-11

Entering Jerusalem, the Lord is surrounded by a crowd who praise Him as the King, quoting the 25th and 26th verses of Psalm 118, "save now ... Blessed is He that cometh in the name of the LORD." Such will be the cry of the nation in a day to come, when a remnant awakened to repentance will look to the LORD for salvation. That time had not yet come. But though the leaders of the nation reject the Lord, the babes and sucklings may render a testimony to His glory (Psalm 8:2). Having entered the city and the temple, everything passes under the searching gaze of the Lord, only to make evident the signs of rebellion, corruption and unbelief — a condition that the Lord refuses to sanction by His presence; thus, at eventide, He returns to Bethany where there were a few by whom He was loved and owned.

VERSES 12-14

On the morrow, returning to the city with His disciples, we read of the King that "He was hungry." He sought fruit on a fig tree, but found "nothing but leaves". May we not say, that with the Lord, it was not only a physical hunger, but a spiritual hunger that sought for some return from Israel for all the centuries of goodness bestowed upon the nation by God? Something that would be fruit to satisfy the heart of God. As in the tree, the Lord found plenty of leaves but no fruit; so in the nation, He found a great profession of piety before men, but nothing in the secret life that would be fruit for God.

How solemn the result! Those who, whatever their religious profession before men, cease to live rightly before God, will be set aside as a testimony before men. Thus the Lord has to say, "No man eat fruit of thee hereafter for ever." This surely is a principle of wide application, for, at a later date, the Lord has to say of the church at Ephesus, that made such a fair show of piety with their works, that their affections were not true to Himself, for He has to say, "Thou hast left thy first love." In result the Lord warns them that He would remove their candlestick. The heart not being right with Christ they would lose their testimony before men — a solemn reminder to us all that the real test of spirituality is not the outward profession of piety before men, but the secret life lived before Christ.

Verses 15-19

Having come into the city Jesus went into the temple, only to find how great had been the corruption of the House of God in the hands of men. That House through which God approaches men, and man can approach God, had become corrupted in the hands of religious professors into a means of indulging their greed. What the leaders in Israel did, it is possible for the leaders in the Christian assembly to do, but for the grace of God. In after years, the Apostle Paul warns us against the intrusion into the Christian circle of men of corrupt minds that "suppose gain to be the end of piety" (1 Timothy 6:5). Again the

Apostle Peter, who presents the Church as the House of God, exhorts leaders to beware of attempting to feed the flock of God for "filthy lucre" (1 Peter 5:2). He also warns us, in his second epistle, that the time will come when men will arise in the Christian circle who "through covetousness" will "make merchandise" of believers. Thus we learn that the flesh never alters. The covetousness that corrupted the House of God at Jerusalem, has intruded with its corrupting influence into the spiritual House of God. So the time has come "that judgment must begin at the House of God" (1 Peter 4:17).

In plain terms the Lord condemns this corruption. The House which, according to Scripture, was to be a house of prayer for all nations, had been made into a den of thieves (Isaiah 56:7; Jeremiah 7:11). The only effect of the Lord's denunciation of this wickedness was to raise the most extreme opposition against Himself. "The scribes and chief priests heard it, and sought how they might destroy Him." And, in our day, in the presence of the corruption of Christendom, those who seek to follow the Lord in making any stand for the truth, will in some measure encounter opposition. "Truth faileth; and he that departeth from evil maketh himself a prey" (Isaiah 59:15).

Verses 20-26

The Lord instructs His disciples in the great principle that enables the feeblest saint to overcome the greatest difficulty and the most subtle opponent. Outwardly all the power and authority of the established order was in the hands of those who were opposing the Lord and His teaching. How then were a few poor fishermen to stand against the wisdom and power of men in high places? The Lord's answer is, "*Have faith in God.*" All the power of those who were represented by the barren fig tree would vanish before the power of God used by faith. The Jewish nation which represented the whole system of the law, loomed large in the eyes of the disciples, even as a mountain that had stood for ages. Nevertheless, though to sight the nation looked so stable and enduring, faith could discern that it was about to be cast into the sea of nations. But though the mountain would be removed, God would remain, the unfailing resource for faith.

Moreover, faith expresses itself in *prayer* to God. But faith in God not only implies that we make known our requests to God, but in doing so, *we look for an answer*. So the Spirit of God by the Apostle Paul can exhort us to pray "at all seasons with all prayer and supplication in the Spirit, and *watching thereunto with all perseverance*" (Ephesians 6:18). Thus we are warned against the formal repetition of general requests.

Furthermore, in prayer, we are warned by the Lord against cherishing revengeful thoughts against those who may have offended, or opposed us. Nothing will so hinder our prayers as unbelief in God — the One to Whom we pray, as an unforgiving spirit to man about whom we may pray. One has truly said that the Lord "joins with believing prayer the need of a tender spirit of forgiveness towards any against whom the heart might retain the sense of wrong, lest the Father's government should be made to remember one's own offences" (F.W.Grant).

13.
The Exposure and
Rejection of the Leaders

CHAPTER 11:27 TO 12:44

We have seen the Lord Jesus presented to the nation as the King — the Son of David, only to be rejected by the leaders who "sought how they might destroy Him". In this portion of the Gospel, the leaders of the different classes that composed the nation, are exposed in their true condition and rejected by Christ.

CHAPTER 11 VERSES 27-33

As ever, the most bitter opponents to Christ are the religious leaders of a corrupted system. The chief priests, the scribes and elders, are the first to be exposed in the presence of the Lord. By the exercise of Divine power and grace the Lord had given sight to a blind man. As the Son of David, He had entered Jerusalem and cleansed the temple. Alas! these religious leaders, thinking only of themselves and their religious reputation, were alike indifferent to the needs of men, and the holiness of God's house. Seeking to maintain their own authority, they were jealous of any action in the religious sphere, apart from their direction. Indifferent to the corruption that existed in the House of God, and incapable of dealing with it themselves, they oppose the One who can, and does, deal with the evil, by raising the question of authority.

The Lord meets their opposition by asking a question as to John the Baptist. Seeing they take the place of religious leaders, can they decide whether the authority for his mission came from heaven or from men? The Lord's question not only demonstrates their incapacity to judge of questions of authority, but exposes their utter insincerity in raising the question.

Their reasoning among themselves, before answering the Lord, proves their utter lack of all principle. Whatever their convictions, they were ready, as a matter of policy to answer one way or the other. But, they judge that either answer might expose them to condemnation from the Lord or from men. Therefore, they fall back on silence, by saying, "We cannot tell." Their hypocritical wickedness being exposed, the Lord refuses to answer their question.

CHAPTER 12 VERSES 1-12

The religious leaders have been exposed as hypocrites, who, thinking only of their own religious reputation, "feared the people", but had no fear of God. The Lord now sets before them, in a parable, the moral history of the nation to show that, as with the chief priests at that time, so, throughout the past, the leaders had always broken down in responsibility. Moreover, looking on to the near future, the Lord foretells the judgment coming upon the leaders and the nation. Like the vineyard in the parable, Israel had been established in a choice land, and separated from the nations by a law which regulated their lives, and, like a hedge, set bounds around them. Moreover, like the place, digged for the vinefat, provision had been made for the nation to bring forth fruit for God.

Further, as with the tower in the vineyard, they were protected from every enemy. Then the nation had been set in responsibility to maintain their unique position and bring forth fruit for God.

In due season, God seeks some return from the nation for all His goodness. Alas! this moral trial of man as exemplified in Israel's history, only serves to prove his utter ruin. Man has no heart for God, even when so richly blessed by God, and when given every opportunity of realising this goodness.

So it comes to pass that every overture on the part of God, in seeking fruit from the nation, is, not only repulsed, but met by increasing resentment. The first servant is sent away empty. The second is treated with insult. Others are sent, and meet not only insult, but persecution even unto death. Increasingly, the nation shows the failure of man under responsibility. But there is one last test, to see if it is possible to act upon the heart of man. There is one Son — the well beloved Son — He shall be sent, and if there is a spark of goodness in the husbandmen, they will surely reverence the Son. There may be cause of dislike and even hatred in the best of prophets and kings, but in the Son there can be no cause of hatred. Alas! He has to say, "They fought against Me without a cause. For my love they are my adversaries … they have rewarded me evil for good, and hatred for my love" (Psalm 109:3-5).

The advent of the Son made manifest the real state of the heart of man. Israel would fain have a kingdom without Christ, and the Gentiles would have a world without God, even as the husbandmen in the parable say, "This is the heir, come let us kill Him, and the inheritance shall be ours." And as it was with the leaders of Israel, in the day of the Lord, so it is with the whole world today. It is increasingly seen that man's will is to shut God out of His own world. The evolutionist would shut God out of His creation; the politician would exclude God from government, and the modernist would shut God out of religion.

Here, then, we are permitted to see the true character of the flesh that is in us. It can be patriotic and social and religious, but if it is allowed to have its own way it will kill Christ and cast Him out of the world. CHRIST — the Christ of revelation (for the flesh can even invent a Christ of its own imagination) — is the real test, and proves that however fair the outward appearance of the flesh at times, at root it is always in deadly opposition to Christ.

This rejection of Christ brings governmental judgment upon the nation, and would lead to others being taken up from whom God will seek fruit. The Lord quotes their own Scriptures (Psalm 118:22, 23) to convict them of their sin in rejecting Himself. By this terrible sin they were acting in direct opposition to God; for the One they were about to nail to a cross, God was going to exalt to the highest glory. Nevertheless, the Lord indicates that the time is coming when a repentant remnant will own that what the Lord has done is marvellous in their eyes.

With the conscience touched, but the heart unreached, man is only maddened. Thus, with these wicked men, they sought to lay hold of Him, but for the moment they are hindered by mere policy, for they feared the people. So "they left Him and went their way." How hopeless the condition of those who deliberately turn their backs on Christ and go their way.

Verses 13-17

The religious leaders of the nation having been exposed in all their hatred of Christ, we are now to see the exposure of the leaders of the different parties, into which the nation had become divided. First there comes before the Lord the Pharisees and Herodians. Though opposed to one another, they were united in their hatred of Christ, and alike in their desire to exalt themselves in this world. The Pharisees were seeking a religious reputation by the outward observance of forms and ceremonies; the Herodians were seeking advancement in the social and political world. Of necessity they both find that One who is here entirely for the glory of God must condemn such aims, and hence they oppose the Lord. All that He was, every truth that He taught, His every act, sprung from motives entirely different to those which swayed the lives of these men. Thus, if they come to Christ, it is not to learn at His feet, but in the hope of catching Him in His words. The worldly motives that swayed them had so entirely blinded them to the glory of Christ, and so puffed them up with the conceit of their own powers, and importance, that they actually thought they could catch the Lord of glory in His words.

Moreover, they think that the tactics that can often be used so successfully with their fellow-men can be used with the Lord. Thus by flattery and falsehood they seek to entrap the Lord. They say, "Thou art true, and carest for no man: for Thou regardest not the person of men, but teachest the way of God in truth." This, though true in fact, was not the true expression of their evil hearts. Having, as they thought, prepared the way by flattery, they put their question, "Is it lawful to give tribute to Caesar or not?" Their wicked minds had devised a question which, they thought, would compromise Him, whatever answer He gave, be it "Yes" or "No", with either Jews or Gentiles.

The Lord exposes their hypocrisy with His question, "Why tempt ye Me?" Seeking to catch Him in His words they fall into their own trap and make manifest their low condition, actually before men, and morally before God. In answer to the Lord's request, a penny is brought to Him, and He asks, "Whose is this image and superscription?" and they said unto Him, "Caesar's." Obviously, then, it belongs to Caesar; that being so it is only right to "render to Caesar the things that be Caesar's, and to God the things that are God's." The Roman power could find no fault with rendering to Caesar the things that are Caesar's; the Jew could find no fault with the principle of rendering to God the things that are God's. The fact that Caesar's money was circulating in the land was a witness to the low condition of the nation in bondage to the Gentile. Alas! in spite of their humiliating position there was no true repentance, for they continually rebelled against Caesar, and they rejected their own Messiah. Perceiving the wisdom of the Lord's reply, they marvelled, but, alas! they had neither conscience toward God nor man.

Verses 18-27

The Pharisees and Herodians having been exposed and silenced in the light of the Lord's presence, the Sadducees now approach the Lord, only to have their ignorance and infidelity laid bare. The Sadducees were the materialists of that day, and represented the infidelity of the flesh. It has been truly said, "The strength of infidelity lies in putting difficulties, in raising up imaginary cases which do not apply, in reasoning from the things of men to the things of God" (W.Kelly). So in this case these wicked men seek to oppose the truth by ridicule. They raise an imaginary case which they judge, shows the absurdity of resurrection. As usual with infidels, they betray gross ignorance of Scripture and ignore the power of God. If Scripture had said that people marry in the resurrection state their imaginary case might indeed have presented a difficulty. If God had no power, the resurrection itself would be impossible.

There is not a line in Scripture to say that the relationships of earth will be continued in heaven. We shall not rise as husbands and wives, parents and children, masters and servants, but in this respect shall be as the angels. We shall not be angels, as people vainly imagine, but like them in being free from earthly relationships. The believer will enjoy privileges, and heavenly relationships far above angels, and the passing relationships of the time state.

As touching the resurrection, the Lord again shows their ignorance of Scripture. They had quoted Moses, in the endeavour to show that the Lord's teaching was in opposition to Moses; the Lord therefore turns to Moses to expose their ignorance of what He had said. Is it not recorded in the book of Moses that "in the bush God spake unto him, saying, I am the God of Abraham, and the God of Isaac, and the God of Jacob." When the incident at the bush occurred, Abraham, Isaac and Jacob had been long dead, yet God still speaks of Himself as their God: He is not, however, the God of the dead, but the God of the living. Though dead to this scene, they still live and will rise again to enjoy the promises of God, which, sin having come in, can only be fulfilled on resurrection ground. Thus the Lord can say to the infidels of that day, as of this, "Ye therefore do greatly err."

VERSES 28-34

The Sadducees are followed by a representative of the Scribes, who were the interpreters of the law, and believed that some laws were of greater importance than others. He asks the Lord to give His judgment as to "Which is the first commandment of all?" In His perfect wisdom the Lord passes over the ten commandments which would naturally occur to the mind of man, and selects certain great exhortations from the Pentateuch which sum up the law and express man's whole duty to God and man.

The first responsibility of man is to maintain the unity of the Godhead according to the Scripture which says, "Hear, O Israel; The Lord our God is one Lord." It follows then, that man is responsible to love God more than himself, and to the exclusion of every other object as a competitor; secondly, to love his neighbour as himself. This is the summing up of the whole law and presents the whole duty of man upon earth according to the law. If these two laws were kept none of the other laws would be broken.

The scribe bears witness to the perfection of the Lord's reply. His conscience tells him that the Lord has expressed the truth. He recognises that to give God His due, and act rightly towards one's neighbour is of more value than all outward forms and ceremonies of the law. As ever, in God's sight, the moral condition of the soul is of far greater importance in the sight of God than the outward show of piety.

The Lord recognises the discreetness of this lawyer. As far as intelligence and an honest recognition of the truth goes, he was not far from the kingdom of God. But, alas! he was outside. He saw the truth of what Christ said, but he did not see the glory of Christ, or bow in recognition of the truth of His Person. As one has said, "Whether a person is near or far off from the kingdom of God, it is equally destructive if he does not enter it" (W.Kelly). As with many others, the lawyer saw what was in the law, but he failed to see his own deep need as one that had entirely failed to meet the demands of the law, and hence he failed to see the glory of the Person of Christ, and the grace that was in Him to meet the need of those who have entirely failed in their responsibilities.

After this, no man durst ask the Lord any question. Representatives of all classes — Priests, Rulers, Pharisees, Herodians, Sadducees and Lawyers — had come with their questions, tempting the Lord, only to find themselves exposed and silenced. The Pharisee, who professed to uphold religion, had not rendered to God the things that are God's. The Herodian, who professed to maintain the political interest of Caesar had not rendered to Caesar the things that are Caesar's. The Sadducee, that boasted in intellect, was remarkable for his ignorance. And the Scribe, who expounded the law, had not kept the law. However opposed to one another, they are all united in opposition to Christ, and in manifesting the complete ruin of man in responsibility.

Verses 35-37

Having answered all questions and silenced every opposer the Lord, Himself, asks a question of supreme importance, for it touches the glory of His Person upon which all blessing for man depends. "How say the scribes that Christ is the Son of David? For David himself said by the Holy Spirit, the Lord said to my Lord, Sit Thou on my right hand, till I make thine enemies thy footstool." The questions of His adversaries had been based on the reasonings and imaginations of their own minds: the Lord's question is based on Scripture, and goes to the root of their solemn position, for it brings to light the mystery of His Person, which they refused to acknowledge. The scribes saw truly that the Messiah would be the Son of David, but they did not see, what the Holy Spirit distinctly states in their own Scriptures, that He was not only the Son of David but also David's Lord. How can He be both David's Son and David's Lord? There is only one answer. He is truly Man, and yet as truly a Divine Person. Refusing to own the truth of His Person they miss the blessing, and the One they reject passes to the right hand of God, there to wait until the time comes to deal with all His adversaries in judgment.

VERSES 38-40

The exposure of the leaders is followed by the Lord's word of warning against those who made a great religious profession, but whose one motive was the exaltation of themselves. Such, love display — "long clothing"; public recognition — "salutations in the market-places"; religious pre-eminence — "the chief seats in the synagogues"; social distinction — "the uppermost rooms at feasts"; self-aggrandisement, even at the expense of widows; and religious ostentation when, "for a pretence" they "make long prayers". How solemn are the Lord's words, "These shall receive severer judgment." The greater the pretension, the greater the judgment.

VERSES 41-44

In contrast to those who have been exposed as religious hypocrites, we are permitted to see that there were those in the nation that the Lord delights to own, represented by this poor widow. The godly remnant that returned from Babylon in the days of Ezra to build the House of God, are still seen in this devoted soul who gave up all her living to maintain the House of God. Ignorant she may have been that this house had been corrupted by man and was about to be destroyed in judgment; but her heart was right with God, and her motives pure. She gave but two mites, but, in God's sight it was more than all others gave, though they cast in much. They gave of their abundance; "she of her want did cast in all that she had, even all her living." God judges of the value of a gift, not by the amount given, but by what is kept back for self.

14.
The Great Tribulation

CHAPTER 13

The low condition of the Jews has been exposed and the leaders of every party condemned in the presence of the Lord. They had rejected, and were about to crucify their Messiah. This supreme wickedness would bring the nation under the governmental judgment of God leading to the great tribulation foretold by the prophets. This would entail difficulties and dangers, suffering and persecution, for the Lord's true disciples — the godly remnant in the midst of an ungodly nation. To prepare them for these terrible days, the Lord alone with His disciples, foretells the course of events, warning them of the dangers to which they will be exposed, and instructing them how to act in the presence of these perils.

VERSES 1-2

This instruction is introduced by one of the disciples calling the Lord's attention to the beauty and magnificence of the temple. The Lord admits that the buildings were great, but, that which is so admired by men had become a den of thieves in the sight of God and was doomed to destruction. Not one stone would be left upon another.

Verses 3-4

This statement that would sound so strange to those who looked upon the temple as the house of God and the glorious centre of their religion, leads one of the disciples to ask, "When shall these things be? and what shall be the sign when all these things are going to be fulfilled?"

In the discourse that follows, the Lord does much more than answer these questions. They were thinking of events, but the Lord had before Him His own and their sufferings and dangers in the midst of the events. Moreover, in the account given by Mark, the Lord, in harmony with the special purpose of the gospel, very specially admonishes His disciples as to their service in bearing testimony to Himself in the midst of the nation by whom He has been rejected.

To understand the warnings and instructions, it is very necessary to remember that the disciples represent the godly Jewish remnant, and therefore the ministry of which the Lord speaks is not distinctively christian ministry in connection with Christianity, though there are many principles and truths that equally apply to both God's earthly and heavenly people. It is a ministry that was commenced by the twelve in the midst of the Jews during the Lord's presence on earth, and, after His ascension was continued amongst the Jews until the rejection of the Holy Spirit at the stoning of Stephen. It will again be taken up by a godly remnant amongst the Jews after the Church has been caught away, and will widen out to all nations. The gospel they preached, and will yet preach, is not exactly the gospel that is preached today. It will indeed be Christ and His work that they proclaim, and the grace of God that forgives sinners on the ground of Christ's work. But it will be the good news that He is coming to reign and that repentance and forgiveness of sins through

105

faith in Christ is the way of entrance into the blessings of the earthly kingdom (Revelation 14:6, 7).

VERSES 5-6

The Lord opens His discourse with five warnings. First, the disciples are warned against false Christs. Many will come in the Name of Christ; some even daring to say "I am Christ", and the Lord adds, that such will "deceive many". This warning proves how distinctly the Lord has in view the godly remnant in the midst of the Jewish nation. Christians, instructed in Christian truth, would not be deceived by a man professing to be the Christ; for they know the next time they will see Christ it will be in the clouds. The godly remnant will rightly be looking for Christ to appear on the earth, and therefore might easily be deceived by the report that He had come.

VERSES 7-8

Secondly, the disciples are warned against concluding that the end is near on account of "wars and rumours of wars". "Such things must needs be" in a world that has rejected Christ. Wars, earthquakes, famines and troubles, are the beginning of sorrows, not the end.

VERSES 9-11

Thirdly, the disciples are warned that their testimony will bring them into conflict with the authorities of the world. But this persecution would be the means used of God to bring the gospel before the great ones of the earth — a "testimony to" rulers and kings (N.Tr.). Moreover, this gospel must first be preached among all nations before the end when Christ comes. In view of this testimony, and the persecution it entails, the Lord instructs His disciples not to be careful beforehand as to what they shall say when prisoners before the great ones of the earth, nor to prepare their defence. It would be given them what to say, in that hour, for they would not be the speakers, but simply the mouthpiece of the Holy Ghost.

VERSE 12

Fourthly, the disciples are warned that the presentation of the truth in the power of the Holy Spirit awakens such enmity in the human heart that persecution will come from natural relations, and the closer the relationship the more bitter the hatred. Brother will rise against brother, father against son, and children will rise up against parents, causing them even to be put to death.

VERSE 13

Fifthly, the disciples are warned that the persecution would not only come from those in authority, and from the closest natural relations, but, they would be hated of *all men* because of their confession of the Name of Christ. But he that endures to the end will be saved — whatever the end may be, whether a martyr's death or the coming of Christ to the earth. As ever, the test of reality is continuance. There may, indeed, be failure, and even the love of many growing cold, but those that are real will endure. Peter broke down, but his faith did not fail; he continued to the end.

VERSES 14-20

In the portion of the discourse that follows, the Lord passes on to speak of events that are yet future. The Church period is passed over in silence, and we learn what will take place at Jerusalem during the time of the great tribulation that will follow the Church interval. This terrible time is definitely foretold by the prophet Jeremiah, who says, "Alas! for that day is great, so that none is like it, it is even the time of Jacob's trouble" (Jeremiah 30:7). Again, Daniel looks on to this time, when he says, "There shall be a time of trouble such as never was since there was a nation even to that same time" (Daniel 12:1). So in the corresponding passage in Matthew 24:21, as well as in this discourse recorded by Mark, the Lord tells us that in the time of this great tribulation there shall be days of affliction "such as was not from the beginning of the creation which God created unto this time, neither shall be."

The destruction of Jerusalem, with all its horrors, may have foreshadowed the future, but in nowise fulfils the prophecy of this time of trouble. We learn from this passage that immediately following the great tribulation, the Lord will come to earth. It is evident that after the destruction of Jerusalem the Lord did not come. Moreover there cannot be two times of tribulation "such as never were". Furthermore, Daniel tells us that this time of trial for the Jewish nation will take place during the reign of Antichrist, who will be received by the nation that has rejected their own Messiah (John 5:43). During the reign of this wicked man there will be set up the most terrible form of idolatry which the Lord refers to as "the abomination of desolation". The effect will be to spread desolation in Jerusalem and Judaea.

The setting up of this abomination will be the culmination of man's hostility to God. It will be the sign that the testimony of the godly remnant is finished, and that they are to flee from Judaea to the mountains. There has been nothing in the past, nor will there be in the future, to equal the terrible afflictions of these days. It will be so great, both for the nation and the godly remnant, that unless the Lord shortens the days no flesh will survive. For the elect's sake the days of this great trial will be shortened.

As ever, the Lord thinks of His own in the midst of trials and afflictions. He warns them, He instructs them, and

He cares for them. He thinks of the workmen in the field and the women in the home, and he is not unmindful of the weather.

VERSES 21-23

The Lord warns the disciples against false hopes of deliverance; against false reports, of false Christs; against false prophets, false signs, and apparent wonders. Their safety will be in remembering the words of the Lord, "I have foretold you all things."

VERSES 24-25

"In those days", following upon the great tribulation amongst the Jews, all established authority among the Gentiles will be overthrown. The order that God has established for the government of the world will fall into confusion. Supreme power, as figuratively set forth by the sun, is darkened. Derived authority, as figured by the moon, ceases to have any influence, and subordinate authorities, likened to the stars, lose their place and power. This dispensation, in spite of all men's boasted progress will end in unparalleled tribulation, confusion and anarchy.

VERSE 26

The wickedness of Jew and Gentile having come to a head, God publicly intervenes by the coming of Christ as the Son of Man to take possession of the earth. His first coming was in circumstances of weakness and humiliation; His second coming will be in great power and glory.

VERSE 27

The gathering together of the elect of Israel dispersed among the Gentiles, will immediately follow the coming of the Son of Man. We know from other Scriptures, that the Church will have already been gathered to meet Christ in the air, and will appear with Him; but of this we hear nothing in this passage. The Lord is speaking to Jewish disciples, and of Jewish hopes, and does not speak of truths concerning the Church and of which His hearers, at that time, could have no knowledge.

VERSES **28-29**

The fig tree putting forth its tender leaves assures us that summer is nigh. So the appearance of the godly remnant in the midst of the apostate nation of Israel will presage the near approach of the time of blessing for the nation.

VERSES **30-31**

The perverse and unbelieving generation of the Jews will not pass away till all these things be done. They may, indeed, be scattered among the nations, with no land of their own, but as we know they have never been absorbed by other nations. Moreover, the Lord's words will not pass away till all these things be fulfilled. We know this must be true of all the Lord's words; but it is specially stated in regard to His second coming because of the unbelief of our hearts as to any intervention of God in regard to the course of this world.

VERSES **32-36**

Of the day of His coming knoweth no man, not even the Son who had become Man. Speaking as in the place of a Servant He could say He knows not the day. Not knowing the day, we are to "watch and pray". Christ is as one who has gone into a far country and given authority to his bondmen and to every man his work, and commanded the porter to watch. Let the Lord's servants watch, therefore, lest coming suddenly He may find them overcome by the world, and spiritually asleep to Himself.

VERSE 37

The Lord's closing words are an exhortation to all His people. All the details of the future may not have an immediate application to Christians, but the closing word to watch is for all. Believers, of every dispensation receive their authority from the Lord, and are the servants of the Lord, each having some work given to them by the Lord. Each one is to beware of falling into spiritual sleep and failing to work for the Lord.

15.
The Shadow of the Cross

CHAPTER 14

With chapter 14, we enter upon the last solemn scenes of the Lord's life, in which many hearts are revealed. The corruption and violence of the Jewish leaders, the love of a devoted woman, the treachery of the betrayer, and the failure of a true disciple, pass before us. Above all there shines forth the infinite love and perfect grace of Christ as He institutes the Supper, faces the agony of Gethsemane, and submits in silence to the insults of men.

VERSES 1-2

The chapter opens with a brief record of the deadly hostility of the leaders of the nation. Already they had compassed the Lord about with words of hatred, and fought against Him without a cause; they had rewarded Him evil for good and hatred for love (Psalm 109:2-5). At every step He had manifested perfect grace; on every hand He had wrought only good. He had healed the sick, clothed the naked, fed the hungry, forgiven sins, delivered from the devil and raised the dead. He had warned these men, pleaded with them, and wept over them, but all in vain.

Thou loved'st them, but they would not be loved,
And human hatred fought with love divine;
They saw Thee shed the tears of love unmoved,
And mocked the grace that would have made them Thine.

Now, at last, the time has come when they are determined to take Him and put Him to death. To carry out their purpose they have to resort to craft, the sure proof that their motives were evil, and that though they may fear men, they have no fear of God. The people, if they had little sense of their personal need of Christ, could at least appreciate His goodness and the benefits of His miracles. Fearing any uproar, when crowds were gathered at Jerusalem for the passover, these leaders decide that they will not take the Lord on the feast day. God, however, had determined otherwise and, as ever, His will prevails in spite of the craft and plots of men.

Verses 3-9

With this brief reference to the leaders we pass to the beautiful scene in the home at Bethany. As the Lord sat at meat, in the house of Simon the leper, a woman, who we know from other accounts was Mary the sister of Martha, brought an alabaster flask of very precious ointment of spikenard and poured the contents on the Lord's head. Mary thus expresses her appreciation of Christ, her affection for Christ, and her spiritual insight. At the moment her intelligence appears to have exceeded that of the other disciples. Won by grace and attracted by love, she had, in other days, sat at His feet to hear His word. As one has said, "The grace and love of Jesus had produced love for Him, and His word had produced spiritual intelligence."

Her love to Christ made her sensible of the increasing hatred of the Jews. Her act was the witness of love's appreciation of Christ at the very moment when the plottings of men expressed their hatred of Christ. Alas! Mary's act of homage brings to light the avarice of some who were present. We know, from the account in the Gospel of John, that Judas was the leader of those who were indignant with Mary. That which was gain to Christ was loss to Judas. Men can appreciate beneficent acts for men, but can see little, if any, value in an act of homage that has only Christ as the object. In like spirit are we not, as Christians, in danger of being rightly active in preaching to sinners and in care of saints, while showing little appreciation for an act of worship that makes everything of Christ? Let us not forget that those who murmur at the devotedness of Mary, in reality put a light upon Christ. If Mary's act is mere waste, then Christ is not worthy of the homage of His people.

If, however, Mary's act calls forth the indignation of men, it draws out the appreciation of Christ. The Lord delights to say, "She hath wrought a *good work on Me*." In Luke 10, we read that Mary chose *"that good part"*. Here, we learn, that she does *"a good work"*. The good part is to sit at His feet and hear His word, the good work is work which has Christ for its motive. There may be much activity in service, but if Christ is not the motive it will have little value in the day to come. Moreover, the Lord not only commends Mary's work on account of its pure motive, but also because she had done "what she could". In service for Christ it is not possible to overlook an opportunity for some comparatively small and obscure act of service, and aim rather at a great public work which, after all, may have the false motive of exalting self. Does not this fine scene encourage us to do what we can, however small the service, with the pure motive of exalting Christ?

Very blessedly, the Lord gives us the true spiritual significance of her act. She had come aforehand to anoint His body to the burying. Others, indeed, will come when it is too late with their sweet spices to express their true, but unintelligent appreciation of Christ. Mary, with greater spiritual intelligence expresses her love before the burial. So great is the value that the Lord sets upon Mary's act that He says, "Wheresoever this gospel shall be preached throughout the whole world, this also that she hath done shall be spoken of for a memorial of her." Her act of love is to be used for all time as a beautiful example of the true and proper result of the gospel. Not only does the gospel bring to us the knowledge of salvation and the forgiveness of sins, but it wins the heart to Christ, so that He becomes the supreme object of life. We know that the Lord's Supper which has been celebrated throughout the ages is a continual memorial of the perfect Saviour and His infinite love to His people; but the one supper that took place at Bethany has become the lasting memorial of a devoted saint and her love to Christ.

VERSES 10-11

The "good work" of Mary is immediately followed by the evil work of Judas. Urged on by the enmity of the devil without, and the covetousness of the flesh within, Judas, without conscience toward God, went to the chief priests to betray the Lord into their hands. They, equally without conscience or fear of God, promised to give him money. To gain the bribe, Judas pursues his evil work of seeking to betray the Lord at a moment convenient to the chief priests.

VERSES 12-16

Unmoved by the plottings of wicked men, the Lord pursues His course of perfect love for His own, and institutes the supper whereby we may all have the privilege of emulating Mary's act of worship. The incidents that prepare the way for the supper, though in themselves simple, bring into display the glory of the Person of the Lord. Two disciples are sent forward to prepare the feast. The Lord is going to death, but, none the less, He is the King with royal rights that can claim the guest chamber, and to whose sovereign will all must submit. Moreover, He is a divine Person to whom everything is known. The man with the "pitcher of water", "the goodman of the house", the "large upper room furnished", are all before His eyes. The disciples going forth to carry out His instructions find all things come to pass as He said unto them.

Verses 17-21

In the evening He cometh with the twelve and they sat down to partake of the Passover — the commemoration of the deliverance of the Israelites from Egypt. The Lord was about to accomplish a far greater deliverance for His people. This eternal redemption necessitates His death which would be brought about through the betrayal of one of the twelve. The Lord, in His perfect love felt deeply that one of those who had lived in His holy presence, heard His words of grace, witnessed His infinite love and patience, should thus act. It was an expression of the anguish of His heart, when He said, "One of you which eateth with Me shall betray Me." The greater and the more perfect the love the greater the anguish in the presence of such a betrayal of love. Never had love in all its perfection been so expressed as in Christ, and never had one lived outwardly so near to Christ as Judas. Yet all in vain, for even if he had any appreciation of the love, he loved money still more. The heartlessness of the betrayal, and its utter wickedness is seen in that the one who was about to betray the Lord could dip with Him in the dish. The Lord would have others to share with Him in His sorrows. It has been said, "He does not proudly hide them", but desires to lay His sorrows as a Man in human hearts; love "counts upon love" (J.N.Darby). The sorrows of the forsaking when upon the cross we cannot share, but these are the sorrows caused by men, into which as men we can, in our small measure enter. But the betrayal of Judas was long foretold: all was taking place "as it is written". But woe to the betrayer, for again it has been said, "The accomplishment of God's counsels does not take away the iniquity of those who fulfil them; otherwise how could God judge the world?" (J.N.Darby).

VERSES 22-24

The institution of the Lord's Supper follows. The words "as they did eat" clearly distinguish between the Passover of which they were partaking and the Lord's Supper. In His supper the bread represents His body; the cup, His blood, shed not for Jews only but for many. It is a supper of remembrance. We are loved with such a love that the Lord values our remembrance of Himself. The blood of Christ in all its infinite value is ever before the eye of God, and He desires that it should ever be remembered by His people.

VERSE 25

The Lord has used the cup as the symbol of His blood shed for many. Looking at the wine in its natural sense as the fruit of the vine, it would set forth earthly joy. The death of Christ breaks His links with earth and earthly, until at last the Kingdom of God is established on the earth. Today the believers' links are with a heavenly Christ Who has suffered on earth; they wait for the future Kingdom to share with Christ in the glories and joys of the earthly Kingdom.

Verse 26

After the supper, having sung a hymn, "they went out into the mount of Olives". The two things are so marvellous. We could understand better His singing a hymn, and remaining in the Upper Room, or going forth without singing. But to sing a hymn when going forth to meet His enemies, the betrayal, the denial, the agony of Gethsemane, and the forsaking of the cross, would prove a calmness of spirit that was surely the outcome of having the Father's will in view and the joy that was set before Him beyond the cross.

Verses 27-31

The very circumstances, however, that reveal the perfection of the Lord disclose the weakness of the disciples. They can sing together in the presence of the Lord, and yet, that same night, when out of His presence they will be offended and scattered. Alas! how solemnly they set forth what has happened amongst the Lord's people. It is only in His presence with every heart engaged with Himself that we can sing together, as the prophet can say, "With the voice together shall they sing; for they shall see eye to eye" (Isaiah 52:8). It is only when every eye is fixed on Him that we shall see eye to eye. Out of His presence we easily become offended because of Christ, and offended with one another, and offended saints will soon part company and become scattered sheep. Never again will the dispersed of Israel, or the scattered and divided church, sing together until they all meet around the Lord and see Him face to face.

But, blessed be His name, He never fails; therefore the scattering will end and the gathering time will come. So in their day the disciples would find, for after He was risen they would learn that the Lord was unchanged in all the love and grace of His heart. He, the great Shepherd of the sheep, would go before them and once again His sheep would follow Him.

The Lord has given the word of warning, followed by a word of encouragement. Alas! like Peter we, too often, are heedless of His warnings, and miss the blessing of His words of encouragement, because of our self-confidence. Ignorant of our weakness we think that we are safe though others may fail. So Peter says, "Although all shall be offended yet will not I." They would all be offended, but the one who takes the lead in expressing his self-confidence would have the greatest fall. We break down in the very thing about which we boast. Peter boasts that he will never be offended. The Lord says, "This night … thou shalt deny Me thrice."

This forecast of his coming failure, only makes Peter more vehement in his protestation of devotedness to the Lord. He says, "If I should die with Thee, I will not deny Thee in anywise." Doubtless Peter was sincere, but we have to learn that sincerity is not enough to keep us true to the Lord. We need to be strong in the grace that is in Christ Jesus if we are to overcome the weakness of the flesh, escape the wiles of the devil and be delivered from the fear of man. All that the devil needs to encompass the fall of an Apostle, when out of touch with Christ, is the simple question of a young girl. Peter's boasting, in which all the disciples join, calls forth no further word from the Lord. Evidently there are occasions when the statements of believers are so manifestly in the flesh that it is useless and needless to attempt any reply. There is a time to be silent and a time to speak.

Verses 32-42

It was a deep sorrow to the Lord that the nation were plotting to put Him to death, that one of the twelve was about to betray Him, that another was going to deny Him, and all would be offended because of Him; but in Gethsemane the Lord faces the far deeper sorrow that He was about to endure at the cross when, made sin, He would be forsaken by God. In the presence of this great sorrow, as in all the other trials of His perfect life, He gave Himself to prayer. But, whatever relief prayer may bring, the immediate effect is to make the trial more acutely felt. Prayer brings all the circumstances into the presence of God, there to be realised in all their true character. The ruin of Israel, the treachery of a Judas, the weakness and failure of His own, the power and enmity of Satan, the reality of judgment, the righteous requirements of a holy God, were surely felt and entered into by our Lord in the presence of the Father.

The Lord takes with Him into the Garden, Peter, James and John — those who in due time will have a special place as pillars in the church. Already they had been the chosen witnesses of His glories on the Mount; now they are given the opportunity to share His sorrows in the Garden. The actual forsaking on the cross, none could share, but in the exercise of soul in anticipation of the cross others can, in their measure, have part. For Him, death was, as our holy substitute the bearing of the penalty of sin, therefore He can say, "My soul is exceeding sorrowful unto death." Having borne the penalty of death, He has for the believer robbed death of its terrors. Stephen can rejoice in the prospect of death, and Paul can say it is far better to depart and be with Christ. It was part of His perfection to deprecate the cross, and therefore He can say to the Father, "All things are possible to Thee; take away this cup from Me." But it was equally part of His perfection to submit to the cross and carry out the Father's will; therefore He can add, "Nevertheless not what I will, but what Thou wilt."

The sorrows of the Garden were too deep, as before the glories of the Mount were too great for poor weak human nature. On both occasions the disciples find relief in sleep. Peter who had gone beyond others in boasting of his devotedness to the Lord, is specially addressed by the Lord when He comes to these sleeping saints and asks, "Simon sleepest thou? Couldest not thou watch one hour?" Prayer, which expresses our dependence upon God, will alone prepare us for coming temptation. The self-confidence of nature leaves us, too often, with little dread of temptation and therefore with little sense of our need of prayer. Yet, with tender compassion the Lord owns the reality of their love for Himself while recognising their weakness; "The spirit truly is ready, but the flesh is weak."

Again, He went away and prayed, only to find when He returned to His disciples that they were still asleep. The Lord's warnings had been unheeded, for their eyes were heavy with sleep. The third time the Lord returns to the disciples, He has to say, "Sleep on now and take your rest." They had missed the opportunity of watching with the Lord and proved their own weakness, and the Lord has to say, "It is enough." The time for watching and praying had passed; the time of trial had come; the betrayer was at hand, and the One who had watched and prayed, can now say in confidence and dependence upon God, "Rise up, let us go."

VERSES 43-45

In the solemn betrayal scene that follows, we see the evil of our own hearts when left to ourselves and hardened by

Satan. Apart from the grace of God how easily we can indulge the flesh, and, giving way to our lusts, come under the power of Satan, leading even to the betrayal of Christ. Thus, with Judas, he can say to the enemies of the Lord, "Take Him and lead Him away safely." It would seem that Judas was mocking them when he said, "Lead Him away safely." Apparently he had counted upon the Lord passing through the midst of His enemies, as on former occasions, and thus the Lord would deliver Himself from His enemies, while Judas would secure the money that he coveted. Knowing nothing of the counsels of God or the perfection of the obedience of the Lord, he was not prepared for the submission of the Lord to His enemies in order to carry out the will of the Father according to the words just uttered in the Garden, "Not what I will but what Thou wilt."

Thus, absorbed with the gratification of his own lust, and blind to the glory of Christ, Judas dares, not only to betray the Lord, but to do so with a kiss. A little later the enemies of the Lord will spit in His face; but with equal grace the Lord submits to the awful hypocrisy of the betrayer that kisses Him, as to the insulting contempt of enemies that spit upon Him. Wonderful Saviour that endured the contradiction of sinners!

VERSES 46-47

But if Judas, the betrayer, was not prepared for the submission of the Lord to His enemies, neither was Peter, a true disciple. His name is not mentioned but we know that it was Peter who drew his sword and smote a servant of the high priest. Moved by lust, Judas betrays the Lord; moved by love, Peter defends the Lord. Nevertheless, in spite of his sincerity, actually Peter was opposing the path of the perfect Servant of Jehovah. No mention is made of the healing of the wound in this gospel, as the leading thought is not so much to present the power of the Lord, but rather His submission as the perfect Servant.

VERSES 48-49

The covetousness of Judas has been exposed, and also the fleshly energy of Peter, who was ready enough to fight, if not to pray. Now the cowardice and meanness of these Jewish leaders is exposed. They could have taken the Lord daily in the temple in an open way, for the Lord had taught openly and publicly, but their cowardly fear of the people, and lack of all principle, led them to act as if they were dealing with a thief. They understood a thief, and how to deal with a thief, but the infinite perfections of Christ were beyond their comprehension.

VERSES 50-52

Further we see the weakness of the disciples. "They all forsook Him, and fled." One, however, ventures still to follow, only in the end to retreat with greater shame.

VERSES 53-65

In submission to the Father's will, the Lord allows Himself to be led away to appear before the Jewish council. Peter with true love to the Lord, "followed Him"; but, acting in self-confidence, he does so without the mind of the Lord, and so follows "afar off". Thus, as too often with ourselves, following without divine guidance, he enters into temptation without divine support, only to learn the utter weakness of the flesh.

In the scene that follows we see, in the chief priests and their council, to what depths of wickedness religious flesh can sink. Already they had determined to put Christ to death; therefore, the trial that follows was not to enquire if He had done anything worthy of death, but rather a horrible device to cover murder with a show of justice.

With malice in their hearts, they seek not the truth, but for witnesses "*against Jesus* to put Him to death". Failing to discover such, they fall back on false witnesses only to find that they will not serve their purpose, for these false witnesses condemned themselves by contradicting one another.

Finally the high priest has to appeal to Christ, Himself. In the presence of all this enmity and malice the Lord "held His peace, and answered nothing". Peter, who was a witness of these solemn scenes, can in later years tell us that "when He was reviled" He "reviled not again". "As a sheep before her shearers is dumb, so He openeth not His mouth" (Isaiah 53:7). To the accusations of malice He had nothing to say; but when challenged as to the glory of His Person, He witnesses to the truth, without hesitation, cost what it may — the perfect example for all His servants. Having failed to carry out their wicked purpose by malicious lies, they now seek to condemn the Lord for witnessing to the truth. All the devil succeeded in doing was to bring to light the truth as to the glory of the Person of Christ and expose the utter wickedness of religious flesh, which if allowed for the moment to accomplish its wicked ends, is only an instrument to carry out God's "counsel determined before to be done".

The Lord Jesus was indeed the Christ, the Son of the Blessed, but He was also the Son of Man who hereafter will be seen sitting on the right hand of power, and returning to earth in glory. Rejected as the Son of God, according to Psalm 2, He takes the place of Son of Man according to Psalm 8.

In the eyes of these leaders, blinded by unbelief, the truth appears as blasphemy, and without a dissenting voice "they all condemned Him to be guilty of death". In perfect submission to the Father's will, the One who will soon be exalted to the right hand of power, and come again in glory, offers no resistance to the outrages of those who spit in His face and smite Him with their hands.

VERSES 66-72

Alas! the Lord has not only to meet the insults of wicked men, but also the denial of Himself by a disciple. The self-confidence of Peter had made him heedless of the Lord's warnings, and neglectful of the Lord's exhortations to watch and pray. The flesh has led him into temptation in which it cannot support him. While the Lord was silent in grace in the presence of the malice of His enemies, Peter was silent in fear as he warmed himself at the world's fire in the company of the Lord's enemies. When the Lord speaks to confess the truth, Peter speaks to deny it. In his self-confidence, Peter had said, "If I should die with Thee, I will not deny Thee." When put to the test by the simple question of a maid, without any suggestion of harm coming to him, still less of death, he scents danger and denies the Lord. But conscience will not allow him to remain in the company of those to whom he has lied. He goes into the porch, and immediately, according to the Lord's warning words, he hears the cock crow. But again the maid sees Peter, and remarks to those that stood by, "This is one of them." For the second time Peter denies the Lord. A little later, others said to Peter, "Surely thou art one of them." Peter not only denies the Lord for the third time, but does so with curses and oaths. How little Peter knew, what we too are so slow to recognise, that "the heart is deceitful above all things and desperately wicked". Deceived by his own self-confidence he failed to realise that such was the desperate wickedness of his heart that cursing and swearing and denial of his beloved Master were there ready to break forth if the occasion arose.

How solemn is Peter's course in these solemn scenes, recorded, not that we should dwell upon his failure to belittle a devoted servant of the Lord, but rather that we may learn the evil of our own hearts and take heed to ourselves. When the Lord warns Peter of his coming denial, Peter, in self-confidence, contradicts the Lord and boasts in his devotedness. When, a little later, the Lord is watching and praying, Peter is sleeping. When, in the presence of His enemies the Lord is dumb, like a lamb before her shearers, Peter is actually smiting with a sword. When the Lord is witnessing the good confession before the high priest, Peter is denying the Lord before a simple maid.

Peter has broken down; but the Lord remains, and the Lord is the Same. The sufferings He endured through being rejected by the nation, betrayed by a false disciple, denied by a true disciple, and forsaken by all could not turn the Lord from His own or wither up the love of His heart. As Peter hears the cock crow for the second time, he calls to mind the word that Jesus had said, "Before the cock crow twice, thou shalt deny Me thrice." These words broke poor Peter's heart and led to tears of repentance. "*When he thought thereon he wept.*" It has been well said, "While watchfulness and prayer are ever needed, he only will be blameless, and shameless, and without offence, who walks in the solemn conviction that he has to fear the outbreak of the foulest sins, unless his soul be occupied with Jesus." We do not know the deceitfulness of our own hearts, for the same passage that tells us it is deceitful above all things and desperately wicked, goes on to ask, "Who can know it?" Immediately, the prophet gives the answer, "I the Lord search the heart, I try the reins" (Jeremiah 17:9, 10). The One who searches and knows is the One who alone is able to keep us from falling, and restore us when we fall. Thus, the restored Peter is brought to confess on resurrection day when he owns, "Lord, Thou knowest all things." No more will he talk about his own heart, and boast about what he will do and not do, but rather will he leave himself in the hands of the One who knows all things — all the evil of our hearts and all the power of the enemy — and who alone can keep us from falling.

> *O keep my soul, then Jesus,*
> *Abiding still with Thee,*
> *And if I wander, teach me*
> *Soon back to Thee to flee.*

16.
The Cross

CHAPTER 15

In the scenes that surround the cross the evil of fallen man is disclosed in all its enormity. Every class is represented — Jews and Gentiles, priests and people, the ruler and his soldiers, the passers by and criminal thieves. However great their political and social distinctions, all are united in their hatred and rejection of Christ (1-32).

When man and all his wickedness is lost to sight in the darkness that covered the land, we are permitted to hear the cry from the Saviour that tells us He was forsaken of God, when, as the Holy Victim, He was made sin that we might be made the righteousness of God in Him (33-38).

Finally, when the forsaking is past, we have a threefold witness borne to the Lord Jesus by the centurion, some devoted women, and Joseph of Arimathea (39-47).

VERSES 1-15

Already the Lord has been unjustly condemned by the Jewish council. But all the world has to be proved guilty; therefore, as the perfect Servant of Jehovah, the Lord submits to appear before the judgment seat of the Roman power, only to prove the utter breakdown of government in the hands of the Gentiles.

Before Pilate, the Lord is again challenged as to the truth, for at once Pilate asks, "Art Thou the King of the Jews?" The Lord replies, "Thou sayest it." As one has said, "Whether it was before the high priest or before Pilate, it was the truth He confessed and for the truth He was condemned by man" (W.Kelly). To the accusations of the Jews, He answered nothing. In the perfection of His way, He knows when to speak and when to keep silence. For the truth He will speak, but when it is a question of meeting personal malice against Himself, He is silent. Good for us to profit by His perfect example, and follow in the steps of the One who, when He was reviled, reviled not again. There is a time when silence will produce a far greater effect upon the conscience than any word that can be uttered. Nevertheless, such silence is entirely foreign to our fallen nature. Thus, Pilate marvelled at His silence.

Knowing full well that all the accusations of the Jews had no real weight as proving any wrong on the part of Christ, Pilate seeks, on the one hand, to appease the Jews, and on the other hand, to escape the infamy of condemning an innocent person, by falling back on a custom at the Feast of the Passover, of releasing "one prisoner, whomsoever they desired". At that time there was a notable prisoner, named Barabbas, who lay bound for rebellion and murder. Encouraged by the multitude who were clamouring for this custom to be carried out, Pilate suggests that He should release Jesus, the King of the Jews rather than Barabbas, the murderer.

To fall back on this custom was a mere compromise, and added to the wickedness of the judge; for if, as Pilate knew, the blessed Lord was innocent, a righteous judgment would demand that, apart from any custom, He should have been released. Moreover the injustice of Pilate in not at once releasing an innocent Man is increased by the fact that he was perfectly aware that, in having bound the Lord and brought Him before the judgment seat, these wicked men were moved by envy. Envy, or jealousy, whether in a sinner or in a saint is one of the greatest incentives for evil in the world. It was envy that led to the first murder, when Cain killed his brother: it was envy that led to the greatest murder when the Jews killed their Messiah. Well may the preacher say, "Wrath is cruel, and anger is outrageous; but who is able to stand before envy?" (Proverbs 27:4). With envy filling their hearts these religious leaders incite the people to choose Barabbas rather than Christ. Moved by envy they reject Christ, the One who is "altogether lovely", and choose a murderer and a rebel. Well for all believers to take to heart the lessons of this solemn scene, and heed the words of the apostle James when he warns us against allowing "bitter envying and strife" in our hearts. If not judged in the heart it will lead to confusion and every evil work, even in the christian circle (James 3:14-16).

Pilate may be a hardened man of the world, but at least he made some feeble remonstrance against the condemnation of the One that all knew to be innocent. Therefore, if he is to release Barabbas he asks, "What will ye then that I shall do unto Him whom ye call the King of the Jews?" Without any hesitation they cried out, "Crucify Him." We do not care for the company of a rebel and a murderer, but such is the enmity of the flesh to God, that, if left to ourselves, and we have to choose between a murderer and Christ, we prefer the murderer.

Again Pilate asks, "Why, what evil hath He done?" Their only answer is the unreasoning cry of a mob, "Crucify

Him." Willing to content the people, he abandons all show of justice, releases Barabbas, and having scourged the One that he knows to be innocent, delivers Him up to be crucified.

VERSES 16-20

In the treatment of the Lord at the hand of the soldiers we see the brutality of man that finds its pleasure in outraging a defenceless person. It was no part of a soldier's duty to maltreat a prisoner, but the lowly grace and perfection of this Holy Prisoner brought God near to them, and this was intolerable to fallen man. The One who will yet be crowned with many crowns at the hand of a righteous God, submits to be crowned with a crown of thorns at the hands of wicked men. He who will rule the nations with a rod of iron, allows poor wretched man to smite Him with a reed. In mockery they bow the knee before the One to whom they will have to bow in the day of judgment.

VERSE 21

The violent soldiers, indifferent to the liberty and rights of others, compel one returning from his labours in the field to bear the cross. Simon the Cyrenian had the honour of bearing the actual cross for the One who suffered on the cross for all the world. God, apparently was not unmindful of this small service for the Lord; for we are told that this Simon was the father of Alexander and Rufus. This seems suggestive of the Rufus mentioned in Romans 16:13, and would imply that Alexander and Rufus were well known converts when Mark wrote his gospel.

VERSES 22-32

No indignity or humiliation is spared the Lord. Having crucified Him in the place of a skull, the soldiers gamble for His clothes. In derision they pour contempt upon the nation by the superscription of His accusation, "THE KING OF THE JEWS", and at the same time crucifying Him between two thieves. Unknown to themselves they were fulfilling scripture which said, "He was numbered with the transgressors."

It might be thought that the passers by would at least refrain from taking part in this terrible scene, but even they wag their heads, rail upon Him, misapply His words, and challenge Him to "Save Himself, and come down from the cross."

The chief priests join with others in mocking the Lord, when they said, "He saved others; Himself He cannot save." This indeed, was true, little as they realised that it was the truth. But what they add is wholly false, for they say, "Let Christ the King of Israel descend now from the cross, that we may see and believe." Faith cometh by hearing not by sight. Moreover, had He come down from the cross belief would have been in vain. We should yet be in our sins.

Finally, the Christ of God is rejected and scorned by the lowest criminals, for we read, "They that were crucified with Him reviled Him."

Verses 33-36

We have seen the Lord rejected by all men from the highest to the lowest, and forsaken by His disciples. Now we are permitted to hear of His far deeper sufferings when forsaken by God. It is no longer the envy, malice, and cruelty of men that He has to bear, but the penalty of sin when delivered up to death by a holy God. Into this solemn scene no man can, or shall intrude. Darkness was over the land. Christ was alone with God hidden from every eye, when He, who knew no sin, was made sin. As made sin He had to endure the forsaking of God. But may we not say that, never was He more precious to God than when in perfect obedience He endured the forsaking of God? He ever glorified the Father, but never in a greater degree than when made sin and forsaken. That such a sacrifice was required magnifies the holy nature of God; that such a sacrifice could be given magnifies the love of God. No less a sacrifice could secure the glory of God or obtain the salvation of men.

But what must it have been to His holy nature to be made sin? Coming into the world He was spoken of as that "Holy Thing": going out of it He was "made sin". The One who was the Object of the Father's delight from all eternity is forsaken. From the twenty-second Psalm, we learn that the One who utters the cry, "My God, my God why hast Thou forsaken me?" alone can give the answer, "Thou art holy, O Thou that dwellest amid the praises of Israel." If the purpose of the heart of God, to dwell in the midst of a praising people, is to be fulfilled, then the holiness of God must first be met. Nothing can meet the holy requirements of a holy God in respect of sin except the offering of Christ without spot.

VERSES 37-38

When all was accomplished, "Jesus cried with a loud voice, and gave up the ghost." His cry with a loud voice proved, indeed, that His death was not the result of the failure and exhaustion of natural powers. One has said, "Jesus did not die because He could not live, as all others do." If the holiness of God was to be met, and salvation to be made possible for sinners, He must die; but no man took His life from Him. He, Himself, gave up His life.

Immediately the veil of the temple was rent in twain from the top to the bottom. The veil separated the holy place from the holy of holies. It spoke, indeed, of the presence

THE GOSPEL OF MARK

of God, but man shut out from God. Such was the character of the time of law. God present but man unable to draw near to God. The rending of the veil proclaimed that all was over with Judaism; but more it tells us that God can now in righteousness come out in grace with the good news of forgiveness for man, and that man can draw near to God on the ground of the precious blood.

VERSE 39

The great work of the cross being finished, the first voice to be lifted up as a witness to the glory of the Person of Christ, is a Gentile, the harbinger of the new day, when a great host from the Gentiles will confess the Saviour as the Son of God. Doubtless, this centurion had seen many a death on fields of battle, but never a death like that of Christ. He recognises that the One who can, with a loud cry, yield up His spirit, must be more than man. Thus, he can say, "Truly this Man was the Son of God."

VERSES 40-41

Then certain devoted women, who had followed the Lord and ministered to Him of their substance, in the days of His flesh, have honourable mention. In love they had followed the Lord in His life of service, they clung to Him in death upon the cross, they behold when His body is laid in the grave. It is easy to dwell upon their lack of intelligence, while falling far behind them in their devoted love.

VERSES 42-47

If when the disciples had fled, these devoted women shine forth in time of danger, so too an honourable counsellor is emboldened to come forward, and beg the body of Jesus for burial. Though a true believer, who waited for the Kingdom of God, yet his high social position may have hindered him from identifying himself with the lowly

Jesus and His humble disciples. But, as so often, the greatness of the evil forces faith to show itself, and those whom we might judge to be spiritually of little account make a firm stand on the side of the Lord, when others that we might expect to take a lead entirely fail.

Thus the word of God is fulfilled that tells us that though men appointed His grave with the wicked, yet He should be with the rich in His death (Isaiah 53:9 N.Tr.). Thus if men are allowed with every insult to nail Christ to a cross, that the counsel of God may be carried out, care is taken — that great work being finished — that His body shall be buried with due reverence, and without further insults from wicked men.

17.
The Resurrection and Ascension

CHAPTER 16

VERSES 1-3

For the third time these three devoted women — Mary Magdalene, Mary the mother of James, and Salome — come before us. Apparently they had already bought sweet spices to anoint the Lord's body when the sabbath was past. Unbelief thought to find the Lord's body in the grave, and ignorance would seek to retain it there. But the Spirit of God delights to take the precious from the vile, and dwell upon their devoted love that led them to purchase the spices and come to the grave at the rising of the sun.

On the way to the grave they say to one another, "Who shall roll us away the stone from the door of the sepulchre?" To the reasoning mind of the natural man, there is still a great stone at the grave of Christ. Alienated from God, fallen man finds insuperable difficulty in the truth of resurrection. The Greek philosophers, as indeed the philosophers of today, may profess belief in the immortality of the soul, but they refuse to accept the resurrection of the body. It is pleasing to the mind of man to think that his soul lives on after it has left the body, but if the body is to be raised it is evident that the power of God must be put forth, and the thought of being dependent upon the God that men hate, is repugnant to the mind of man. Leave God out and resurrection is impossible, bring in God, and His power, and all difficulties vanish — the stone is rolled away.

VERSES 4-7

Coming to the grave these devoted women find that God had been before them, and the stone is rolled away; not indeed that the body of the Lord might leave the grave, but that disciples might enter in and see that the place where He had been laid is empty. No stone, however great, could hold the body of the Lord in the grave.

Entering the grave they are at once confronted with a heavenly messenger to assure their hearts, and calm their fears, as he tells them, "Ye seek Jesus of Nazareth, which was crucified; He is not here; behold the place where they laid Him." They were seeking Jesus, and this being so, in spite of much ignorance and unbelief, all would be well. What are we seeking? Is Jesus the object of our hearts? As one has said, "It is the consecration of the heart to the Lord that brings light and intelligence to the soul" (J.N.Darby). How often our blindness to truth and inability to distinguish between right and wrong can be traced to our lack of the single eye that has Christ as the One Object. We often seek our own will, and exaltation, rather than "seek Jesus" and His glory. The measure in which we "seek Jesus" is the measure in which we get light. We may seek many things that are good in themselves but short of Jesus: we may seek souls, seek service, the good of man, and the welfare of the saints; but, if we "seek Jesus" all else will fall rightly into its place and we shall find light for our path. Seeking Jesus, these women receive light from heaven and are sent on a service for the Lord.

They were to deliver this message to "His disciples *and Peter*". It is touching to notice that in the gospel that so fully gives the details of Peter's grievous fall, we have this special mention of the name of Peter. Had the message been simply to the disciples, Peter might have said, "It cannot include me, I am no longer a disciple." Any such thought is dispelled by the special mention of Peter's name. The disciples are to learn that though they had all forsaken the Lord and fled, and though Peter had denied Him, yet the Lord's heart of love is unchanged towards them, and, as in the days of His life here, so now in res-urrection, He will "go before" His disciples to lead the way, and they will "see Him", and all will come to pass "as He said". May we not say, in a wider sense, that in spite of the ruin of the church in responsibility, the scattering and failure of God's people, the time is coming when He will gather all His sheep together around Himself, our risen and glorious Lord, and we shall see Him face to face, and every word He has uttered will be fulfilled.

VERSE 8

They had seen the empty tomb, they had listened to the angel, but Jesus they had not seen; as we read in the gospel of Luke, "Him they saw not." Apart from Christ, Himself, the great stone rolled away, the empty sepulchre, the vision of angels, only leave us trembling and amazed.

VERSES 9-11

Now we learn that already the Lord had appeared to Mary Magdalene out of whom He had cast seven demons. The one who was a witness to the Lord's power over demons, now becomes a witness to His power over death. She car-ries the glad news that the Lord is risen to the disciples as they mourned and wept. Alas! though they heard the message, they believed not.

VERSES *12-13*

The brief reference to the Lord's appearance to the two disciples on the way to Emmaus tells that neither was their witness believed.

VERSES *14-18*

Finally we have the record of the Lord's appearance to the eleven, as they sat at meat. The Lord upbraids them for their unbelief which is traced to the hardness of their hearts. Cannot much of our unbelief be traced to the hardness of our hearts that, so often are unresponsive to His love and unimpressed by His word?

In spite, however, of this exposure of their hearts, the Lord immediately sends them forth to preach to others. We might think that such unbelief and hardness of heart would be a proof that they were entirely unfitted for the service of preaching to others. But this very exposure of their hearts in the presence of the Lord was a preparation for service. It is when we find out something of the true character of our hearts, and learn our own nothingness, that God can take us up for blessing to others.

They were to go into all the world and present the gospel to every creature. "He that believeth and is baptized shall be saved; but he that believeth not shall be condemned." It would be contrary to the truth to deduce from this passage that baptism has any saving power before God, for the essential truth is believing the gospel. Therefore, it is not said, "He that believeth not, and is not baptized shall be condemned." As one has said, "Unbelief was the fatal evil above all to be dreaded. Whether a man was baptized or not, if he did not believe, he must be condemned." Baptism has this importance that it is the open sign before men of the faith before God. The man who professes to believe and yet refuses to be baptized is practically seeking to hide his profession of faith in order that he may keep in with the world. We may well question the reality of that man's faith. The true believer will confess his faith by separating from the world. Baptism is the sign of death, the great separator. By being baptized the believer leaves the world to come into the Christian sphere on earth amongst God's people.

The Lord tells His disciples that signs should follow them that believe. In Christ's name they would cast out demons, speak with tongues, and heal the sick. It is to be noticed that the Lord does not say that these signs would follow *all that believe*, or that they would continue for *all time*. It is well to distinguish between the sign-gifts referred to by the Apostle in 1 Corinthians 12:29, 30, and the nourishment gifts of Ephesians 4:11. The sign-gifts in Corinthians were given to the early church for a public testimony, to attract the attention of an unbelieving world. The gifts for the nourishment of the body came from the ascended Head. Seeing that the church has entirely broken down in responsibility, the Lord ceases to call attention to a ruined church by outward and miraculous signs. But though the church is shorn of her outward ornaments, the Lord does not cease to love and nourish His body; thus the gifts of Ephesians go on to the end.

Verses 19-20

Having given His commission to His disciples, the Lord was received up into heaven to take His place on the right hand of God. His work on earth as the perfect servant is finished. Nevertheless, He works with His disciples, confirming the word they preached with signs following.

THE GOSPEL OF MARK

OTHER BOOKS BY HAMILTON SMITH

"THE LORD IS MY SHEPHERD" AND OTHER PAPERS

    ISBN 978-0-901860-06-4; Scripture Truth Publications

    97 pages; Paperback; July 1987

ELIJAH: A PROPHET OF THE LORD

    ISBN 978-0-901860-68-2; Scripture Truth Publications

    Paperback; March 2007

ELISHA: THE MAN OF GOD

    ISBN 978-0-901860-77-4; Scripture Truth Publications

    Paperback; March 2007

www.ingramcontent.com/pod-product-compliance
Lightning Source LLC
Chambersburg PA
CBHW051832040426

42447CB00006B/483